Quest
in the Caribbean

Book Four
of the
Quest Series

David Beaupré

Published by buddha bees

**Cover Design and Cover Photo of Quest in Nevis
by David Beaupré**

Quest in the Caribbean
© 2016 David Beaupré

Published by buddha bees

"The sea has been kind to us. It has been our home, a very strict master and unforgiving teacher. We also learned a great deal about each other and what it takes to be good companions on a tiny boat."

Quest in the Caribbean is a work of non-fiction. All places, characters, and events are real. In some cases the names of characters have been altered.

ISBN-13: 978-0692590614   **buddha bees**

ISBN-10: 0692590617

Introduction to Quest in the Caribbean

The final book in the Quest series is 'Quest in the Caribbean'. Wendy and I have become full time sailors. The sea has been kind to us. It has been our home, a very strict master and unforgiving teacher. We slowly learned our lessons of seamanship one day at a time. But more importantly we learned a great deal about each other and what it takes to be good companions on a tiny boat. 'Quest for the Caribbean' begins on a beautiful day in the British Virgin Islands. When we pass through the dangerous, narrow, reef-strewn passage in Virgin Gorda and enter the Caribbean we are just one boat length closer to fulfilling our dream. There are many more islands to explore and miles to sail before the journey is complete. Some of the wonders that await our eager eyes are Saba, the fabled 'island in the clouds' and the neighboring island of Statia. The serenely beautiful island of Nevis, Montserrat's volcanoes, the gentle people of Dominica, Saint Lucia and the Grenadines all enrich our lives. 'Quest for the Caribbean' ends on the south shore of Grenada as we are about to fulfill a destiny that was many hard years in the making.

Introduction to The Quest Series

My wife and I are very fortunate to have followed a path in life that brings us closer to our dreams and to each other. It's nice work when you can get it. From the day we met, our lives have been filled with extraordinary experiences. Somewhere in a lifetime of memorable adventures we purchased a classic sailboat. Little did we guess the implications of preparing Quest and her crew for a life on the ocean. Learning our lessons along the way, Wendy and I were slowly transformed into sailors. From launching Quest in north Florida to a Category 5 hurricane in Grenada, we discover that the art of living on a sailboat is much more than rum-infused beach parties. It was hard work to have fun. But when all the chores are done and the storms have passed, Wendy and I consider ourselves fortunate to have fulfilled our dreams. Everyone can learn to be the master of their destiny. If time does not permit you to sail the ocean blue, I offer you this four book series on how two friends found happiness in their personal quest for paradise. The Quest Series is a true modern sailing story. Come along, let's take this extraordinary journey together.

Introduction to Quest and Crew

How many people have dreamed about sailing away and leaving it all behind? Here's how it happened. 'Quest and Crew' is the first book of a four book series. The story begins hours before a devastating Category 5 hurricane obliterates the south shore of Grenada. It's a story about the many twists and turns that life can take. The sailboat Quest gained a new lease on life with a complete retrofit in the backwoods of North Carolina. The job of the crew becoming real sailors began in North Palm Beach. On a clear starry night, we left South Florida on a hope enveloped by a dream. Finding ourselves at the beginning of a new adventure, we set sail and anchored one island at a time through the Bahamas. The Caribbean is a few books away. Here is a glimpse into the powerful attraction of sailboats and sapphire water. 'Quest and Crew' is all about the joy of success as well as what it takes to overcome the occasional disaster. From beginning to end, the book is about transforming a rookie crew and beautiful old boat into a sailing adventure. Come for the hurricane, stay for the story.

Introduction to Quest on the Thorny Path

Not all trips to paradise are smooth sailing. 'Quest on the Thorny Path' is the second book of the Quest series. Leave the laid back cruiser hangout of Georgetown, Bahamas behind and hit the big ocean waves for the first time. From Georgetown we take the path less traveled through the deserted out islands of the Bahamas. After a short stay in the Turks and Caicos we follow a route along the north coast of Hispaniola that Christopher Columbus appropriately named the 'Thorny Path'. The book is a true adventure about overcoming fear and dangerous challenges in one of sailing's harshest proving grounds. Bashing through heavy seas and strong headwinds on a lee shore isn't for everyone. But at least you can read about it.

Introduction to Quest for the Virgins

Find our crew poised and ready to venture into the dreaded Mona Passage between Hispaniola and Puerto Rico. We're on our way for a long, leisurely sail on the beautiful south coast of Puerto Rico. It is my pleasure to have you come along for the third book in the Quest series. Included in the itinerary is Vieques, St. Croix, St. John and a little Virgin Gorda. With a unique perspective for the almost unnoticed, 'Quest for the Virgins' will deliver a less common experience of a most popular place. Be whisked away to warm tropical destinations for a humorous glimpse into the life aboard a sailboat in the Caribbean.

David Beaupré
Fall River, Tennessee

Contents

One

The Last Virgin

It was a pleasant and calm morning in Robins Bay, Virgin Gorda in the British Virgins Islands. It was the time of the great morning pause, the calm before the charter boat storm. Soon the fleet would awaken and make their choreographed sprint across the Sound to the accompaniment of five hundred fume belching outboard engines. The daily game of musical chairs at the resorts would then begin.

Fleeting thoughts passed through my mind as I warmed my hands on a mug of tea. The nostalgic question of 'how did I get here?' seemed rather insignificant to the more appropriate question of 'how do I get out of here?'. Wendy and I had been laying low in a small, out-of-the-way anchorage in Virgin Gorda waiting for a favorable wind. With a cooperative wind, we would leave the opulence of the British Virgin Islands and sail south-east to the magical island of Saba.

Making a sailboat a home can be a mind altering experience. Each day, subtle changes occur to create a new you. One's confidence and boating knowledge slowly increase until one day you find yourself a sailor.

Quest in the Caribbean

Unconscious changes begin to steer your actions like the unseen winds. A task which seemed impossible to perform just months ago will be executed flawlessly without the least thought. It may take six months, maybe a year. Eventually if you make it through the break-in period, you will become a different person. The many subtle changes that take place compound and to your delight you will soon be living the life that you dreamed about. It is a very big change that many people crave.

It was June 1st in the Caribbean, the first day of hurricane season. For many people in the northern hemisphere, June ushers in warm days, pleasant nights, and blossom scented breezes. It is a time of great joy. For boat owners in the Caribbean, the pleasures of summer can be overshadowed by the specter of hurricane season. Very few liveaboards in the Caribbean are immune to the fear of coming face to face with a major hurricane. It is a sobering thought. I would rather be thrown into a cage with an eight hundred pound Bengal tiger than try to survive a hurricane on a sailboat. At least with a big cat I may have a chance to talk my way out of it. 'Here kitty, kitty'.

If you wish to avoid hurricanes in the Caribbean it is prudent to follow a popular yet simple hurricane avoidance strategy. Get thee below 12° south latitude and stay there until November. Being safely moored in south Grenada for the hurricane season was our mission as well as our mantra. Within a few hours we would be acting on that plan by making our night passage one hundred miles due southeast to the island of Saba. A few more hops down the island chain and we would be safe.

The Last Virgin

I shook off the thought of hurricanes and leaned back into the cockpit cushions with a warm cup of tea and contemplated the immense natural beauty of North Sound. Quest was anchored alone in a small, deserted bay on the southern shore of North Sound. She was a comfortable distance from the many resorts. Any boat in Virgin Gorda Sound that isn't tethered to a mooring ball in front of a restaurant, bar, scuba shop or yacht club is an outsider. It isn't easy and it takes a bit of doing but we managed to find solitude in the world's most populated charter boat haven.

The phenomenal attraction of the BVI as a destination for vacationers and yacht charters is relatively recent. The Arawak Indians turned the islands into their private cozy resort around 400 BC. For two thousand years they flourished and built a sophisticated civilization. Then Columbus plundered by around 1493. His arrival heralded the beginning of the Caribbean land grab. Columbus immediately claimed the islands by the right of 'ordinary discovery' in 1493, thinking that they were part of a Japanese archipelago. Through the centuries, the islands have passed through Spanish, then Dutch, and finally British hands. Each nation endured tremendous hardship in their efforts to tame the Virgins. Their best efforts only managed to produce pitifully marginal plantations. The soil is poor. The climate is harsh. A few hundred years of failed agricultural attempts gave way to the more lucrative enterprise of the slave trade.

The Virgins in the 1800's were not the playground of the wealthy as they are today. The islands were hell on earth for their occupants. Disease and poor nutrition claimed most colonists within a few years. No European in their right mind willingly relocated to the Islands. It was a place of banishment for the British landed gentry's ne'er'-do-well sons. Convicts, murderers and thieves avoiding the British gallows comprised the second tier of society. At the bottom of the food chain were the pirates, slave traders and finally the black slaves. Time has greatly improved the standard of living in the Islands. Malaria and yellow fever are eradicated and they have air-conditioning.

Trip planning for our over night sail from Virgin Gorda to Saba was very straightforward. The distance between the two islands is approximately one hundred miles. The wind was expected to be fifteen knots accompanied by a five foot long period ocean swell. We could expect a beautiful broad reach under a starry sky. If we averaged 5.5 knots of speed, it would take Quest approximately eighteen hours to sail to Saba from Virgin Gorda.

When anchoring in a unfamiliar port for the first time, arriving during daylight hours is always preferred. This avoids the embarrassing midnight question of 'hey, are you sure this is Saba?'. We also had another important wrinkle to consider in our trip planning strategy. It was absolutely necessary to leave Virgin Gorda as close to 12 o'clock noon as possible. A near perfect view of the bottom is essential to navigating a tricky reef passage. This is only possible when the sun is at its zenith.

While making our southerly departure from Virgin Gorda, we would need to pass through a very narrow opening in the reef about a half mile due northeast of Saba

Rock. The reef channel is a tight squeeze for anybody. It is off limits to bare boat charters. The navigable water in the cut through the reef was roughly twenty feet wide and about ten feet deep. Passing a twelve foot wide boat through a twenty foot wide hole of jagged coral is dicey enough. Of greater concern was the three knots of flood current passing through the reef combined with a stiff on shore breeze. Any uncontrolled drift could cause disaster.

The navigational challenges and hazards of the narrow reef channel are easily mitigated by using simple precautions. Make the approach very slowly and only at noon when the contours of the bottom can be seen in high relief. There was one further detail to consider while passing through the narrow cut in the reef at high noon. During the very busy lunch time rush, there would be about two hundred tourists seated on the verandas of the Saba Rock Resort and the Bitter End Resort. These two resorts, which lie on opposite sides of the south side of the Sound, have a spectacular view of the reef. Grounding Quest would be a catastrophe for Wendy and me. It would also provide spectacular entertainment for the resort guests during their noon repast. We would do our absolute best to disappoint them.

It was ten o'clock. We had two hours before anchor up. This gave me plenty of time to prep a light meal which I could serve at sundown.

"Hey Wendy, is there a jar of tahini left in the locker? I'd like to make some hummus."

"That sounds good. I know exactly where it is" she yelled back from the saloon.

I dropped into the galley, pulled the pint sized Cuisinart from under the saloon table and placed it on the table.

"OK, where is it?" I said while looking down and grinning at Wendy who was kneeling on the cabin sole.

Most of the contents of a locker were spread out the length and breadth of the cabin sole. There were plastic boxes filled with engine parts, bags of dehydrated vegetables, bottles of wine, toilet paper, and assorted nick-knacks.

"So you know exactly where the tahini is?" I laughed.

"Yes, I know exactly where the tahini is. Don't distract me" she said studying the detailed map of the locker's contents.

Wendy was Quest's quartermaster. This is probably the least glamorous job on a sailboat. It is also one of the most important. If supplies can be tracked and found easily, it enriches the lives and safety of everyone aboard. There was literally not a single item – not a bolt, manual, or can that was brought aboard Quest which Wendy didn't record on the manifest. The items were then placed in water proof plastic boxes, stowed in a locker, then added to the 'manifest locator map'.

Any small boat has incredibly limited storage space. Every single thing that we owned had to be stored in a space smaller than a modest sized kitchen. Good organization or lack thereof can make your life on a boat easy or very difficult. Wendy adapted very naturally to this aspect of liveaboard cruising. She had literally mapped and accounted for every square inch of space throughout Quest's lockers. She could put her finger on a spare engine zinc as fast as an alternator belt in an emergency.

"Here it is" she said handing the jar of tahini to me.

Finding what you are looking for in the labyrinth of boxes and lockers is only half the job. Putting everything back in its assigned place is the other half. Wendy spent the next ten minutes carefully re-stowing every item back in the water tight boxes. Then each box was dutifully stacked in its assigned space in the locker. Finally she stood beside me while I blended the hummus in the Cuisinart. With a dramatic flourish she placed a line through the word tahini on the detailed manifest of the restocked locker.

"See, it's simple" she said with a grin.

"Organizing the toilet paper is harder than sail handling in a gale" I joked.

"I wouldn't know. You know I don't know anything about sailing" she said.

"You know Wendy it's amazing how ubiquitous hummus has become in America" I said as I added the onion powder.

"It wasn't so very long ago that if you asked for hummus in a store, they brought you to the gardening department" she said.

In the last twenty years, hummus spread across the American landscape like an obsession. What a world we live in – Middle Eastern ethnic food on the shelves of Piggly Wiggly in Mississippi. It seems so out of place. But there it is, pork rinds and kosher hummus living side by side in harmony in Dixie. Who could have guessed the geopolitical implications of the 'hummusization' of the American Deep South? A food that doesn't contain sugar and absolutely cannot be deep fried.

There is one possible explanation for the popularity of hummus. Those ubiquitous twelve ounce, flat plastic containers of 'fresh' hummus that sell for $5 contain about 5¢ worth of ingredients. With a profit margin of about one thousand percent, it was just a matter of time before big business would spread hummus across the American landscape.

The ingredients for hummus consist of four simple and easily acquired ingredients: chickpeas, garlic, tahini and lemon juice. If you ever wish to make your own hummus, begin by soaking a cup of chick peas (aka garbanzo beans). After a night of soaking in salted water, boil the beans or pressure cook them until tender. When they have cooled slightly, place the cooked chickpeas, two rounded tablespoons of tahini, a pinch of spice, a small clove of garlic and a tablespoon of lemon juice in a Cuisinart and blend until you have reached a desirable constituency. To serve, spread on a plate and top with a sprinkle of olive oil if desired. Hummus is a convenient, easy to make, high caloric, protein-packed, nutritionally balanced food that doesn't get any cheaper.

With the addition of a few fresh vegetables and crackers, we had a tasty supper waiting for us. Wendy watched patiently as I scooped the hummus into a storage container.

"Do you remember the first time we ate hummus together?" she said touching the back of my right hand.

I reached up and stroked her shoulder.

"Of course" I said. "It was in the Muslim Quarter of the old City of Jerusalem the morning after we first met. The old Mufti showed us how to get there. You thought I was crazy to bring you to a hummus restaurant for breakfast."

"I can still remember the old man grinding the chickpeas in the kitchen. His ten year old grandson brought the hummus out to us still warm on a platter with onion slices and a couple of fresh pita breads" she said.

"Eating hummus for breakfast sure is a habit in the Middle East. I remember it like it was yesterday." I opened the refrigerator and placed the container of hummus at the top. "I don't have any onion slices for tonight" I said.

"Good" she said. "I never liked the raw onion. I just ate the onion that first morning because you did."

"Are you glad you came with me that morning?" I asked.

"I guess so. It sure beat looking for a McDonald's in the Old City" she laughed.

The clock was rapidly winding down on our stay in the British Virgins.

"It's eleven thirty. Let's raise the anchor and hit the trail" I said.

Within ten minutes the anchor was locked at the bow and we began motoring toward the mooring field in front of the Bitter End Yacht Club. As we put Saba Rock to port, I called Wendy to the wheel.

"You steer. Pay close attention to my hand directions. This cut is going to be tricky" I said.

I walked to the bow and looked at the reef that stretched for a mile in front of us. There was only one opening wide enough and deep enough to sail through. A well chosen waypoint would bring Quest's bow within fifty feet of the correct cut. From my vantage point at the bow, the opening in the reef looked impossibly small. I looked back at the cockpit.

"Here we go. Slow down, watch your drift and don't take your eyes off my hand signals."

As we crept forward, I could feel the sweat rolling down my back. I looked behind me at the Saba Resort. A crowd of people were watching our every move. 'If we hang up on this reef, it's going to be quite a show' I mused to myself.

"Keep coming" I called to Wendy.

I motioned with my right hand indicating a minute course change to starboard. The reef was so close on both sides of the boat that I could have reached out and touched it with a boat hook. The stern cleared the reef. Wendy let out a cheer. Quest was in the Caribbean.

Two

Wrong Way Wendy

Accepting life's threatening situations is an integral daily part of being a sailor. How successfully you react to these constant challenges define your fitness as a sailor. Not everyone aboard a small sailboat needs to feel the weight of constantly striving to make the right decision. After all, a boat can have only one captain. The crew of any boat, large or small, is a cooperative. Skills come together. They gel or they don't. When self interest is put aside for the greater good of arriving safely at a destination; there is harmony. Aboard Quest we had excellent harmony most of the time. In my experience this is a remarkably high success rate for a married crew. How lucky can you get? We are both heavyweight scrappers that don't give up easily. But in our favor, we are most resilient to each others comments and we don't hold a grudge.

We were very happy to have slipped through the Virgin Gorda reef with ease. Returning to the cockpit, I brought the binoculars to my eyes and looked astern. As we gained distance from the reef, the cut seemed to vanish. I scanned the shore line of the Saba Rock Resort. The small crowd that gathered to watch our back door exit from the Virgins had returned to their merry making.

Quest in the Caribbean

When we motored out of the lee of La Gorda, I raised the main and both headsails. Quest surged forward and seemed to take flight into the blue, blue Caribbean on a southeasterly heading of 120°. We were beam reaching in warm trades that held at a constant 15 knots. Looking far out along the waves, the sea looked corrugated by a very long, five foot ocean swell that was undisturbed by even a single whitecap. These were ideal conditions for Quest and her crew. I tightened the main sheet. Her speed increased to over six knots with a comfortable 25° heel. Quest has a very low free-board at the cockpit. With our current heel, I could reach out and touch the larger wave tops as they passed the gunwale. Quest was indescribably beautiful as she pressed through the sea with both headsails raised and drawing. Power, grace and purpose were hers.

There was only one thing that could make this picture better. It was hummus time and beer thirty. While I gave the sails a final trim, Wendy kept herself occupied plating dinner. She reached up from the galley and handed me two platters. One platter was spread with hummus and the other with a selection of carrot sticks, celery and a handful of Triscuits. I took the platters from Wendy and leveled them against the boat's heel on the cockpit table with a bath towel.

We silently munched our vegetables and dipped our hummus to the sounds of water rushing against the hull, wind whistling in the rigging and a light string quartet playing on the cockpit speakers. At that moment the world was all embracing. Eating a simple plate of hummus with a strong boat pulling us to an anticipated destination was one of those elusive moments of joy that makes life complete.

We sat on the lee side of the cockpit and watched the sun dip into the western ocean. The brilliant orange of the setting sun turned to crimson then finally to violet. Then it was gone. We were alone once again in the darkness on a big sea.

"Why don't you get some sleep?" I said to Wendy. "How about if I wake you around 9 o'clock?"

"Nine sounds good to me. I'm really tired" she said turning around and descending the companionway.

After Wendy had settled onto the lee saloon settee, I rigged the sails for night sailing. The jib was furled tight. The smaller staysail was left up and its loose lee sheet cleated tight. This would prevent the staysail from flapping if the wind shifted. Quest was wisely built with a double sheeting system for the main. A ring was bolted on each side of the cabin top. Both port and starboard main sheets ran through independent blocks and tackle which were attached to the rings. This double sheeting system provides incredible strength and security. It doesn't make tacking easy but it is very strong rigging in heavy sea conditions.

When the trim looked as good as it could get, I leaned back into the cushions behind the helm and listened to the quite predictable squeaks and groans from the autopilot's hydraulic ram. The sea and wind held constant. Quest settled into a smooth, predictable soporific sway.

I closed my eyes and thought about the first time that Wendy and I had seen the island of Saba. On an occasion when we flew into St Maarten, we had the pleasure to meet a couple from the lovely island of Saba.

"I bet that you've never heard of Saba" the wife said to us shortly after introducing herself.

"No I haven't" I said, following her lead.

"Not to worry" she said in a Dutch accent. "Not many people have heard about the best island in the Caribbean."

Wendy and I became enthralled with her elaborate description of the island.

"When you go to Saba, you absolutely must fly in. Don't take the ferry from St Maarten" the husband added. "Flying in is half the fun of going."

"Why is that?" I asked.

"You're just going to have to see for yourself" he said with a mischievous glint in his eyes.

It didn't take much persuading. As soon as we arrived at our guesthouse, Wendy booked us a flight to Saba.

A few days later we were making our approach into the most notorious airport in the Caribbean. The Yrausquin Airport is built on the northeast corner of the Dutch island of Saba.

The two ends of the runway each literally begin at the cliff's edge. One step past the white painted line at the end of the runway and you will plummet straight down a cliff. The north length of the runway is built on a precipitous drop off to the Caribbean. Directly north of the runway are cliffs rising several hundred feet to the island's interior. In summary, the Yrausquin Airport is surrounded on all sides by hazards that can easily turn a twin turbo prop plane into a crumpled fireball. On normal

14

days, the trade wind howls across the airport like a freight train. Despite being considered the absolutely most dangerous airport in the Caribbean, it has never suffered a single fatality.

Wendy and I were seated in the first row of the twin Otter turbo STOL (short take off and landing) plane. No sooner had we left the airport in St Maarten when we sighted a small green dot in the distance surrounded by crashing, white foaming waves.

"Look, that's got to be Saba" I said to Wendy.

The island slowly grew larger until it looked no bigger than the back of my hand. The runway wasn't even visible. There were a few bumps and thumps before the cockpit door was thrown open and locked in the open position. This seemed rather unusual. 'This is a strange time to open the door' I thought.

Then the calm, self-assured Dutch voice of the pilot spoke over the cabin speakers. "This is your pilot speaking. We are on our final approach to the enchanted island of Saba. Looking at today's manifest, I think that there may be some people aboard who have not had the pleasure of landing on one of the world's shortest commercial runways. I'll leave the cockpit door open. Feel free to look through the windshield."

Fifteen heads swiveled in unison towards the cockpit door.

"Final approach" the co-pilot said in a mechanical tone.

We were about a thousand feet from the runway.

"I can't believe this" Wendy said. "The runway looks like a driveway."

Everything in my being was telling me that this plane could not possibly stop in that short a distance. We dropped lower and lower to the level of the runway until it seemed as if we would slam directly into the cliff in front of us. The landing gear locked into position. The plane buffeted slightly from side to side as the wings caught an updraft from the cliff. The pilot throttled back on the powerful turbo props and the wheels touched the ground. We were now moving very fast and approaching the end of the runway at an alarming speed. The pilot took his hand from the throttles and adjusted the propeller angle to reverse thrust while at the same time he hit the brakes. The nose of the plane dipped and the G-force slammed me against the seat belts. We came to a stop twenty feet from the end of the runway. There was only the view of the whitecapped Caribbean hundreds of feet below the cockpit windshield. It seemed like we were teetering over the edge of a cliff. Yet, every single person on the plane cheered. As the co-pilot turned the plane around and taxied to the hanger, the pilot looked over his shoulder and glanced into the cabin.

"Good fun, eh?" he said with a huge smile on his face.

Very few things can prepare you for a landing at Yrausquin Airport, with perhaps the exception of landing a jet on an aircraft carrier.

We spent a very pleasant few days enjoying the absolute solitude of the island. Saba has none of the glitz that is so prevalent in the Virgins. It is a place of quiet solitude and meditation where the inhabitants have a very curious way of speaking softly.

'It would be hard to forget Saba' I thought leaning forward on the cockpit cushions to check the time on the instrument cluster. The wind was holding very steady at about fifteen knots with only the occasional errant gust to give the auto-pilot any challenge. It was coming up to 9 o'clock. The moon was high and bright. Our course was 120 degrees. I woke Wendy to take her watch.

"Anything going on?" she asked as I lay down on the warm settee.

"Everything's perfect" I said as the light went out.

I suddenly awoke with a strange dream playing in my head. I dreamed that Quest was spinning. Placing my cold hands in the pockets of the windbreaker, I tried to shake it off. 'Wait a minute' I thought. 'Why am I not on the lee settee anymore?' I reached out and felt for the saloon table. Sure enough, I was still on the starboard settee, but Quest was definitely healing to port. My sleepy mind struggled to make some sense out of the impossible. We were heading south. The wind was from the east. We have to be on a port tack, right? I was fully awake when the engine started. Why would Wendy start the engine? Did the wind shift? I sat up and pulled on a dry pair of socks, walked over to the navigation table and looked at the compass. It read 300°. Either it was a dream or we were off course by 180 degrees. It was real.

"We're headed in the wrong direction" I hollered as I raced up the companionway and into the cockpit. "What's going on?"

Wendy was steering Quest. She had that scared look in her eyes.

"Why are you steering? Why aren't we on autopilot?" I said.

"The autopilot is broken" she said.

"Broken? Broken? What do you mean broken?"

My mind was reeling from a collection of conflicting facts.

"Let me take a look" I said looking down at the compass. "Why are we headed north?" I demanded.

Wendy shrugged.

"How could you possibly not know that we're heading in the wrong direction?"

"No we're not. We're on the right heading. See the compass? I'm holding 120° just like you told me to" she insisted.

"You're reading the compass backwards, WENDY. We're on a heading of 300°. You're exactly 180° off course."

I looked to the fore deck. Sure enough both the main and the staysail were backed. I gave the wheel a strong pull to port. Quest rotated 180° then smartly assumed her original trim and speed. I turned the engine off and reset the autopilot.

"I'm telling you the autopilot's broken. I tried ten times to get it to work" Wendy continued to protest.

"Do you really think that the autopilot is going to

acquire when you are off course by 180°?" I shouted loud enough to be heard in Saba.

Wendy immediately dropped face down into the cockpit cushions.

I went to the galley and poured two fingers of Dominican rum and threw it back. Then I poured another finger.

"Drink this" I said.

"Straight? Do we have any fruit juice?" she asked.

"No, this is not a piña colada. Just drink the rum!" I said with an edge of exasperation to my voice.

After about an hour of interrogating Wendy, between her bouts of weeping, we slowly reconstructed a possible explanation for her less than lackluster performance. Apparently, shortly after I had retired to the settee, the wind temporarily became variable. Wendy was daydreaming at the helm. The autopilot was still engaged and holding course dead-on. For a moment or two the wind shifted slightly. Then a stronger gust of wind caught the headsail and pushed Quest hard to starboard. Wendy panicked, over compensated and turned the wheel hard enough to port to cause the autopilot to disengage. In the darkness and confusion she became even more disoriented, letting go of the wheel. The force of the strong wind caught the luffing sail and swung Quest wildly to starboard. Wendy only regained control of Quest after she had swung all the way around to 300°. Despite the sails being very poorly trimmed, Quest assumed a beam reach exactly 180° off course. Desperately attempting to make any sense of what just happened, Wendy looked at the compass and saw

120° on the back side of the compass card. She was reading the compass backwards. Thinking that she had brought Quest onto the correct heading, she tried to set the autopilot. Autopilots normally won't acquire a destination if the course is off by more than 15°. This is normal and is meant to prevent mechanically caused accidental jibes.

When my blood pressure was finally out of the red zone and the mood on Quest was more cooperative, I looked at Wendy.

"I can understand how you could get scared and spin Quest around in the middle of the night. I can understand how you could get confused when you looked at the compass and read 300° for 120°. There might even be some ridiculous reason why you didn't see that the sails were backed."

"That's great" she said. "I knew that you would finally see it my way."

"I'm not quite close enough to see it your way yet. Answer just one question with a good answer and I'll be happy. How could you not notice that the full moon was on the wrong side of Quest when you performed this feat of navigation?" I said.

"The moon? Oh, the moon. Now that's about as silly as it gets. Do you think that I had time for moon gazing? I was pretty busy when the autopilot broke."

Three

Saba

The wind slackened slightly from midnight onward. Quest managed to maintain her course using conventional navigational techniques. I did my best to keep the mood light in the cockpit by telling a few jokes.

"Wendy, do you know why the chicken crossed the road twice?"

"No, and I don't want to know."

"Well, the chicken crossed the road twice because it's autopilot was broken. Here's another. What did Wrong Way Corrigan's wife ask him every time he returned from a scheduled flight?"

"Did she say, shut-up creep?" Wendy asked.

"No it wasn't quite that droll. Every time Wrong Way Corrigan came home from a mission, she would ask 'So did you get anywhere today honey?'"

"How about a nice cup of tea?" Wendy asked changing the subject.

"Sure" I said.

"With the usual, sugar and rat poison?" she asked.

"Actually, just make it a warm mug of diesel and two spoons of drain cleaner."

Ten minutes later Wendy returned to the cockpit with a mug and handed it to me. I smelled before sipping.

"This is Earl Grey. I asked for diesel fuel" I said.

"You know everybody goofs up from time to time. Even you" she said.

"That's entirely true. I've definitely goofed up a few things. I was just able to fix them. On Quest it's largely irrelevant who goofs things up. The only thing that matters is that I'd be lost without you" I laughed.

"Oh boy. Is this when we both sing 'I Got You Babe' ♫?" she asked.

The matter was considered dropped, at least for a short while.

Our early morning intention was to sail directly for the west coast of Saba and pick up a mooring ball provided by the Saba Conservation Foundation. Anchoring a cruising boat off Saba, even in the designated areas, is very difficult. The cliffs meet the sea almost the entire way around the island. From the edge of the rugged, cliff fringed shoreline the bottom drops off precipitously. Most cruisers find it much more practical to pick up an overnight ball than take their chances anchoring on this underwater drop-off.

When the dark purple of false dawn cast a glow on the eastern horizon, we caught our first glimpse of Saba ten miles directly in front of Quest. The first sight of land from a sailboat can evoke a whole array of emotions. It's often an exciting and powerfully inviting experience. Saba was far from inviting. Saba is a very unique island in the Caribbean. The name 'Saba' is thought to be derived from the Arawak word for rock. Most people who see Saba for

22

the first time will readily agree with the Arawak's descriptive name. The island is so imposing and unapproachable that Columbus actually sailed past without making any attempt to land or harass the natives in the name of church and country.

In the ten million years that breakers have crashed against the shores of Saba, they have barely made an impression on the hard, volcanic rock cliffs that jut straight up to dizzying heights. Tree clad Mt Scenery in the center of the island rises to over 1500 feet. Our first sight of Saba was that of a huge looming darkness. It was anything but a palm fringed island in paradise. The spooky silhouette of the island seemed to absorb light as it blotted out a portion of a starry cloudless night. The closer we sailed, the more it felt as if the island were about to swallow us. The first sight of Saba filled me with dread. Saba is no ordinary island.

The rays of the rising sun soon caught the foggy, mist shrouded peak of Mt Scenery.

"Take the binoculars. Can you see the red signal at the top of the mountain?" I asked.

"It's faint but I think I see it" Wendy said.

The day after we had flown into Saba, we set out on an adventure to climb Mt Scenery. The trail head began close to our rented cottage in the village of Windward Side. The steep, winding muddy trail which leads to the summit passes through tropical forests so dense that they obscure all views of the island as well as the Caribbean. Many small streams cross the rugged trail which zigzags up the mountain. As we climbed higher and higher up the side of the mountain, the temperature dropped significantly and the humidity rose. When we entered the clouds about five hundred feet from the summit, a profound silence enveloped us. The sounds of birds, the snapping of twigs, even the sound of the wind in the trees was muffled by the cloud. Arriving at the summit, we labored to breathe in the soupy air. We both swung around in unison when we heard a man clear his throat.

"Hello" he said getting up from a bench.

"Don't get up. We'll join you" I said.

"I'm Hans" he said.

I made our introductions.

"Do you live on Saba?" Wendy asked.

"Oh no. I live just outside of Amsterdam in the Netherlands" he said. "It's been my dream to climb the highest mountain in the Netherlands since I heard about Mt. Scenery when I was a young boy."

"So you finally made it to the top" I said.

"Yes finally" he said.

What do you say to somebody that waited fifty years to climb a mountain and when he gets to the top he can't see ten feet in front of him? "Not much of a view today" I said stumbling for words.

"No view" he agreed. "When I climbed a low peak in the Alps with the wife in '86, the cloud cover was even worse than this. That's life at the summit. The next year we climbed to the base camp of Everest. That was a climb. The air was so dry and clear that the mountain shimmered. You climb the mountain, you take your chances. That's life!" he said with a shrug.

24

Saba

Wendy nudged my leg. "I'm getting cold. Let's go down" she said.

"Are you coming with us?" I asked Hans.

"No. No, you two go ahead. You don't want an old man slowing you down" he said.

"Maybe we'll see you at the top of another mountain some day" I said getting up.

"I think this is my last mountain" he said.

As we started our long trek down the muddy trail, I caught the faint sound of Hans humming a song to himself. I turned around. Hans was already enveloped by the dense clouds on the mountain top. His haunting melody seemed to be coming from everywhere and nowhere as we made our way down the trail and back to our cottage.

There are many islands in the Caribbean which attract visitors for their active nightlife. Trinidad could easily be classified as the 'party island'. The party on Trinidad has been going nonstop for several generations. Except for a short pause between seven in the morning and lunch time, the party in Trinidad is a permanent lifestyle. Unlike Trinidadians, the wonderful people of Saba do not work hard into the night to perfect the art of playing. In comparison the night life in Saba is slightly less lively than an Irish Wake and slightly more active than a country pub on a Wednesday night.

Wendy and I were thinking soft chair and a bottle of wine rather than a party after we climbed down from Mt. Scenery. We purchased an appropriate South African vintage and some fresh produce from a shop owner in Windward Side.

"You have a tremendous selection of wine for a small store" I said to the shop keeper.

"Yes" he said returning to what he was doing.

'He's being positively gabby' I thought to myself. "Lived on Saba very long?" I asked.

"Yes, very long" he replied.

I paid the grocery bill and we started back to the cottage.

"We might have gotten his name in a couple of days at that rate" I said to Wendy.

The people of Saba are as unique as their Caribbean island. The shop owner wasn't being rude, standoffish or unapproachable. He was being appropriate.

What makes Saba so unique is its paradox. It is controlled by the sea yet it is isolated from the sea. The people of Saba are controlled by the sea because everything must be imported. Even their drinking water in the dry season comes from the sea. In every respect, the population of Saba is married to the sea. Where the paradox is most evident is that although they are irrevocably connected to the sea, they live separate from the sea. The people of Saba literally live in the clouds. The ocean is never more than a few miles from any place on the island. Yet they live on cliffs hundreds of feet above the sea. Only the very agile of foot go out of their way to have direct interaction with the blue Caribbean that surrounds them. The people of Saba live so high up that not even the sounds of the sea penetrate into their snug world. It is a very quiet place. The two main towns of Windward Side and The Bottom are nestled high up in the mountains. There are many places in both towns where one can get a view of the ocean but the ocean does not dominate as it does on most islands in the Caribbean. Saba feels more like a tropical version of Switzerland rather than a typical Caribbean landscape.

The naturally reserved Dutch personality and perspective seem a perfect match for the quiet and solitude. After a very good night's sleep in the mountain air, we waited for the morning sun to take the chill from the night. We tightened our shoe laces and set off for a walking tour of Saba. Even Wendy couldn't get lost on Saba. Just to be sure, we asked the cottage owner how to get to The Bottom.

"Follow the main road out of town. A right turn will take you down to the airport. If you go left, you'll reach The Bottom after a couple of miles" she said.

"How long does it take to walk to The Bottom?" I asked.

She smiled "Don't know. It depends on how fast you can walk." She looked us over. "Could take a while" she said.

The road from Windward Side to Bottom is a windy, mountainous road that is more reminiscent of the dry, hilly country of the north Mediterranean region. Drought resistant ferns, flowering grasses and low shrubs grow in scattered clumps on gray, rocky volcanic hillsides. For a good part of the way to The Bottom the road follows the contours of a high ridge. Each turn and dip along the road afforded us brief views of the blue, white-capped

Caribbean hundreds of feet below. To our right, the ever present cloud shrouded Mt. Scenery. Arriving at the hill overlooking Bottom, we stopped for a bird's eye view of the village before we started our way down. The architecture in The Bottom and all over the island seems to conform to an unwritten code. Roofs are red and walls are white. But instead of giving the impression of sameness and uniformity, the identically colored buildings evoke a feeling of solidarity and community. The village of The Bottom has about 500 residents. It is also the home for the Saba University School of Medicine.

After a thorough fifteen minute tour of The Bottom, we decided to continue our downward spiral following the very steep switchback road which leads out of town and directly to Fort Bay. Fort Bay is the only marine harbor on the island. The temperature increased with every step we took down the steep road to the port. We were tired and drenched with perspiration by the time we reached the crescent-shaped harbor.

"That was a good three hour stroll. How long do you think we'll take climbing back up the hill?" I said.

"I don't even want to try" Wendy replied.

"In that case, let's stand on the road and see if we can get a lift" I said.

We walked to the shoulder of the road. In the distance, I saw a man get into a government vehicle by the breakwall. He drove up and opened the window.

"Need a ride? Hop in" he said removing some paperwork from the seat and dropping it behind him.

"I'm David and this is my wife Wendy."

He thrust out his hand with a smile. "I'm Bram."

"Bram?" I said.

"Yes. Bram, short for Abraham. It's a common Dutch name. I work for the Saba Conservation Foundation. The SCF looks after the marine and land parks on Saba" he said, shifting into low gear for the steep climb up the hill. "Where are you going?"

"Windward Side."

"Windward Side, good" he replied. "That's where I'm going. My wife has lunch ready. Have you been enjoying our beautiful island?" he asked.

"Very much. We're quite impressed" I said.

"Saba is so different from any other island in the Caribbean" Wendy added. "What's it like living here?"

"I like it. But I've never really been anywhere" he said with a laugh. "I go to St. Maarten a couple times a year. What make Saba so different is that there is only about 2000 people living on about five square miles. We're like one big family."

"One big happy family?" I said probing.

He took his eyes off the road for a split second to look over at me. "Happy family? You've got to be kidding. I wouldn't go quite that far" he said.

I was about to let the matter drop when he continued.

"I'm forty-five years old. When I was a kid, Saba seemed so isolated. It's much less so today with computers and the Internet. Being this isolated we develop very strong bonds as well as long lasting conflicts. The Dutch have always had strong opinions. We all know that we have to work together to survive on this rock. But everybody on Saba has their own idea of what 'work together' means."

We were approaching the outskirts of Windward Side.

"You can drop us off here" I said.

"Do you have a couple of minutes?" he asked. "I'd like to show you something."

"Certainly" I replied.

We drove through Windward Side and traveled north towards the airport. Bram pulled over to the shoulder and turned his engine off when we got to Zion's hill overlooking the airport.

"Look at the road going down the hill to the airport. Very steep, eh?" he said.

"Yes, we took this road when we came from the airport" I said.

"How do you think that road was built?" he continued with pride and enthusiasm. "Around 1935, the people of Saba thought they needed a road down this hill and then eventually an airport down there on those flats. Dutch engineers said it couldn't be done. So a carpenter named Josephus Hassell volunteered to take a civil engineering course with the purpose of planning and building the road. That was in 1938. In 1947 the first vehicle ever to come to the island drove up this road. Look down there. This hill goes practically straight down and the road is about two miles long. But here's the most interesting part of the story. The road was built completely by hand. Can you imagine that? No heavy equipment, just men with picks, shovels and wheelbarrows. My father worked on this road. Just about every man on Saba worked on this road. It just looks like another mountain road. But picture looking down this mountain side and having the courage and self-assurance to learn civil engineering from a book and then go build one of the toughest roads in the Caribbean. After they completed the road to the flats they continued and finished the road that you walked on today to get to Fort Bay. It was an unimaginable enterprise. We take a lot of pride in our two lane mountain road, a road that experts said couldn't be built."

Four

No Balls

The night gave way to a warm tropical morning as we sailed into the lee of Saba's west coast. We were becalmed. The engine was started. Except for an avoidable 180° fun-filled midnight jibe, we sailed a straight rhumb line. The high looming cliffs of Saba presented an imposing and magnificent gray-black-green rock wall as we motored closer and closer to Ladder Bay.

"Are you sure that Ladder Bay is where the mooring balls are?" I asked as we approached the waypoint.

"The cruising guide mentions that the overnight mooring balls should have a yellow band" Wendy said.

"You take a look. You've got a good eye for balls" I said.

"I see some kelp over there. But I don't see any yellow balls" Wendy replied. She went to the bow and scanned the area. "No balls" she yelled back to the cockpit grinning.

I turned on the VHF radio and turned to channel sixteen.

"Come in Saba Marine Park. I can't find your balls at Ladder Bay."

I took my hand off the mic. Wendy and I looked at

each other and both laughed. After we composed ourselves, I keyed the mic again.

"Saba Marine Park, come in. Where are the moorings?"

I received no response.

"It's only 6 o'clock David. They're probably still asleep" Wendy said.

"You're probably right. Let's get out of here. This place doesn't have any balls anyway" I said laughing and spitting up a mouthful of coffee.

I put my mug down and raised the main and jib. We pressed further on until we came to the southern shore of the island.

"Maybe there are some balls we can grab at Fort Bay" I said with a straight face.

It was Wendy's turn to cough up coffee. We were sleep deprived and getting sillier by the minute. Everything was uproariously funny.

I swung Quest in very close as we approached the crescent shaped harbor of Fort Bay. The trade wind came shrieking out of the east.

"I see the balls" Wendy said holding the binoculars to her eyes. "They look about a quarter mile due east of Fort Bay."

I had my hands full holding Quest in this wind.

"Take a look at the ocean swell where the balls are" I said.

"Very big swell" Wendy observed.

"OK, come to the cockpit. I'm making a course change. We're going to Oranjestad on St Eustatius" I said.

From the southern tip of Saba, we could just make out a peak on St Eustatius about twenty miles due southeast.

"I was looking forward to lying down and getting some sleep. It looks like we have another five or six hours to go."

"I'll add the waypoints and advance the course to Oranjestad" Wendy offered.

"Good" I said.

The wind was extremely close to the nose as we pulled away from Saba.

"Wendy, I'm making a tack" I said as I turned the wheel to put us on a port tack.

The sails were trimmed for a strong breeze and the lines were squared away. Wendy had booted the laptop and brought up the charting software.

"Take a look at this Wendy. If the wind holds steady from due east, we should be able to make Oranjestad in three, maybe four tacks. Enter these points. When you're done, activate the autopilot. I'm going below to make breakfast" I said.

"Jawohl meine Kapitän. Food good" she said saluting.

Foods of all shapes and descriptions made their way around the ancient world by ship. In 1589 the explorer and adventurer Sir Walter Raleigh brought the first potato to Ireland by ship. The tomato conquered Italy in 1548. Despite the universal, modern day appeal of old world foods like potato, tomato, corn and hummus, there is a food that is even more ubiquitous than all four of these foods combined. You may not find fresh tomatoes in a small village store in the Bahamas or Idaho potatoes in a corner store in Beirut. You won't find hummus on shelves in Syndassko, Siberia. But you will find Ramen noodles in Beirut, even in Syndassko or a small one room store in the Bahamas. According to the World Instant Noodle Association, 100 billion servings of Ramen noodles are consumed each year world wide. The Japanese consider Ramen noodles to be their greatest invention of the 20th Century. Then again, the Japanese voted the Karaoke machine to be their second greatest invention of the 20th Century.

Those ubiquitous 4 x 5 x 1 inch rectangles of dehydrated curly noodles start out much the same way as all noodles. A thick dough made from flour, water and salt is extruded through a shaping die. The one difference with Ramen noodles is that the extruded strands are then fried in hydrogenated palm oil. Voila, deep fried noodles. For twenty centavos a package, Ramen noodles may very well be the most brilliant star in the processed food firmament. They could very well outshine the potato chip.

The real magic with Ramen noodles begins when you open the package and throw out the shiny foil flavor sac that snuggles innocently up against the noodles. Throw it in the garbage before you are tempted to use it. Then make your own broth. You will be happy that you did. The secret to making a homemade soup base to complement the noodles is to begin with vegetable stock (meat stock for carnivores). A supply of canned vegetable stock is an essential in any kitchen for times when it isn't practical to boil up a kettle of vegetables for broth.

Even a good packaged vegetable broth needs enhancing. Pour thirty-two ounces of vegetable broth in a large pot. Add a tablespoon of tamari sauce (soy sauce), a tablespoon of minced onion and a tablespoon of onion powder or Mrs Dash. Bring it to a simmer and turn it off. You now have the most basic of broths steeping on your stove top. This is just the beginning. While it steeps, scour the kitchen for any food that catches your fancy. In my case any vegetable, fresh, canned, frozen or dehydrated will suffice. Canned beans of every color and shape are always a good addition. Fresh carrots, celery, broccoli are great. But don't limit yourself to these obvious choices.

I turned the contents of the refrigerator onto the counter. Within the recesses of the fridge I found two forlorn carrots, a quarter head of lettuce in good shape and a quarter onion. I sliced the carrots about ⅛ inch thick, diced the lettuce and onion very fine and then added everything to the pot. The stove top fiddles were tightened to keep the pot stable while we tacked. The flame was turned to low. Before long the pot was simmering. I tasted it. It was remarkable in its blandness.

I took a second look through the refrigerator. There it was, one of the premium Ramen noodle broth ingredients. Smooth or crunchy, peanut butter is a very powerful enhancement to a broth or sauce. Be careful with peanut butter. Add small amounts at a time until you get the desired flavor. Besides peanut butter being a strong flavoring ingredient, it is an even stronger thickener. I re-tasted the broth. It was good but it still lacked something. I found just what the soup needed in the spice cabinet. A teaspoon of mild Madras curry powder was added to the pot. The only remaining step was a three minute boil on the noodles.

"How far are we from the next tack?" I yelled up the companionway.

"One hundred feet" Wendy replied.

'One hundred feet, oh brother'. I raced up the companionway stairs.

"Thanks for the warning" I said. "Prepare to tack."

The sheets were loosed. The wheel was spun smartly to starboard. Quest swung through the wind. Wendy cleated off the jib while I trimmed the main.

"Lunch should be ready" I said.

"I'm pretty hungry. We haven't eaten since last evening" Wendy said. "I mean, except for the pretzels I ate on my watch."

"So that's what happened last night. You lost control of Quest when you were scarfing pretzels." I said.

"That is absolutely not true. The pretzels had nothing to do with the autopilot breaking. No way. But it could have been the peanut butter."

"What!" I said.

"The pretzels were stale so I went to the galley and got the peanut-butter."

"So Quest jibed when you were in the galley?" I asked.

"No, certainly not. When I was spreading the peanut butter on the pretzels, a piece of pretzel broke off and landed on the cockpit floor. When I bent over to pick it up, the wind gusted. When I looked up Quest had swung hard to starboard. That's when I corrected our course."

"Corrected our course? You mean you pretzeled our course. So the truth finally comes out. It was the peanut butter and pretzels that broke the autopilot!" I said.

"Exactly. Now you've got it" she replied.

I shook my head and returned to the galley.

"I think you're going to like this" I said handing up two bowls of steaming Ramen noodle soup through the companionway.

"I'm sure" she said dipping the spoon into the bowl and tasting the broth. "Wow, this is great. The peanut butter is a very nice touch" she said.

By nine o'clock we had make the final tack on our approach. Oranjestad Bay lies on the lee side of Saint Eustatius. Dropping the main I started the engine and motored into the harbor. At a quick glance, the anchorage seemed calm and tranquil. Wendy looked at the cruising guide.

"There's supposed to be anchoring over there" she said pointing to a spot close to shore.

I dropped the anchor in twenty feet of water.

"Back down hard" I called to Wendy after letting out one hundred feet of chain.

The anchor immediately pulled free. I pulled the chain back up with the help of the windlass and tried again. We had no luck on the second, third or fourth attempt.

"OK" I said taking Quest's wheel. "Look in the guide. Are there any other options?"

No Balls

"There's supposed to be an overnight buoy somewhere over there" she said pointing in the direction of a breakwall.

"Let's give it a try" I said turning the bow.

"There it is" Wendy said.

The green algae covered ball was very hard to see.

"Good job spotting it. Bring us up good and slow" I said extending the boat hook to its full length. "Put Quest in neutral" I shouted when we were ten feet from the mooring.

I caught the pendant after a couple of clumsy tries. The slimy mooring pendant was temporarily slipped over the starboard bow cleat while I prepped a bow line on the port cleat. I fed the bow line through the eye on the pendant and tied it off.

"Back down and give the buoy a good tug" I said returning to the cockpit. "Don't turn the engine off. I'm running the water-maker."

Water-makers are incredible luxuries on a cruising sailboat. Being able to make fresh water from salt water is better than magic. Water is scarce in the Caribbean and very expensive. The bigger problem is that you are never exactly sure what you are buying. Purchased water is often drawn from questionable municipal water supplies. If you won't drink the tap water in a restaurant in Dominica, why would you want your tanks filled with the same water? By the time that this municipal water is delivered to your boat it could have been contaminated in any number of ways. I've seen water delivered to sailboats in 5 gallon used diesel jerry cans. 'Sure mon we cleaned dem real good'. Once bad water is introduced into your on-board water tanks you will have a problem that may take weeks to discover and weeks to remedy. Contaminated tanks will need to be drained and sanitized. It is a big job that you can avoid with a water-maker. If money can be budgeted for a water-maker, it is a very worthwhile purchase.

After we were content that the buoy would hold, I left Quest in reverse gear with the engine on with the dual purpose of completing the water-maker cycle and testing our mooring. My first impression of the Oranjestad Bay was very favorable. On the chart, the harbor looked well protected from the Atlantic. The surface in the anchorage had a light swell that didn't seem out of the ordinary. We were moored close to the shoreline with a spectacular view of the charming old city of Oranjestad. Everything seemed to be perfect until I turned off Quest's engine. As soon as the engine sputtered to a halt, our comfortable conditions rapidly deteriorated from very good to very bad.

With the engine running in reverse there was enough prop wash to keep Quest facing into the small surge coming from outside the anchorage. The moment that I stopped Quest's engine, the boat began turning. Every small wave that struck Quest nudged her a little further to starboard. Within a minute or two, the swell was hitting Quest directly broadside. Quest slowly began to rock lazily from side to side. Wendy climbed through the companionway groggy eyed.

"What's going on? Did a work-boat pass by?" she asked.

No Balls

"No, I don't know what's going on. The swell doesn't look bad at all" I said.

This was a very practical lesson in how the unseen underwater forces can act on a boat. The wave surface that you see on the ocean or in a harbor contains only a tiny part of the total energy that influences the movement of your boat. Most of the energy is below the wave. The waves in Oranjestad Bay seemed almost insignificant. The tremendous turbulence that was beginning to rock Quest was just below the calm surface. Quest has a deep heavy long keel. The unseen forces under the water applied tremendous energy against this very large surface. When your boat is parallel to a bad swell, the simplest solution is usually to lay a stern anchor. An anchor is tied off to a stern cleat. It is dinghied behind the boat and set where it can keep the boat pointed ninety degrees to the surge. Alas the Oranjestad Bay was too congested with small work boats to allow a stern anchor to be deployed. We would somehow have to get used to the roll.

Quest's roll grew worse. Then it became exaggerated. We sat in the saloon looking at each other wondering what was rocking the boat. Our first reaction was to laugh at the exaggerated roll. The laughter quickly turned to frowns of disbelief. This was no ordinary roll. It was unimaginable. The mast of Quest was a giant pendulum whipping back and forth, thirty degrees to starboard, then thirty degrees to port. Back and forth it snapped with the consistency of a clock. "Tick tock, goes the clock, and now what shall we play♫?" Books flew from shelves, lockers swung open then slammed shut. Cans, spares, and shoes rolled back and forth on the shiny cabin sole. *Tick Tock*, our normal world had gone mad in the matter of minutes. I looked through the starboard porthole. Quest's rail was under water and the deck awash with every roll. We slumped to the floor and grabbed the table wedging our feet against the opposite side of the settee. It was like being on a seesaw. One second I was high and looking down at Wendy then it was Wendy's turn to be two feet above me. This was very uncomfortable and getting unnerving. Something had to be done.

"Maybe it a good time to get in the dinghy and check in with Statia customs" I said.

Five

Rock and Roll

With both hands firmly gripping the stern pulpit I tried to keep my balance against the force of Quest's roll. The bow of the dinghy crashed into the metal struts of the port davit as Quest rocked violently to port. After two seconds Quest rolled 45° to starboard. The dinghy slapped the water and bounced straight up narrowly missing the side of my head. This was not going to be a routine dinghy launch. While Quest was in the mid cycle of a roll and relatively horizontal I quickly reached into the raised dinghy and grabbed the dinghy's painter. The painter was then uncoiled and carried around the outside of the stanchions to the port side where it was tied mid ship.

"Wendy can you get up here and give me a hand with this? Hold this line" I said uncleating the starboard davit. "Hold it tight" I said as I reached over and untied the port davit line. I held both lines when they were freed. "Stand back" I said as I simultaneously let go of the lines and gave the dinghy a great shove. The dinghy swung out from the stern and hit the water with a smack sending a wave into the cockpit. "Pull the dinghy alongside and jump in. I'll pass you the motor and gas. Be careful."

Placing the gas on the starboard rail I stumbled back to the stern rail and loosened the 2.5 horsepower Johnson outboard attached to the pulpit. By now Wendy was drifting fifteen feet away, tethered to Quest by the painter. The dinghy floated tranquilly only occasionally disturbed by the waves that Quest was creating.

"It's a lot nicer in my boat" Wendy said as she pulled the dinghy towards Quest.

I handed her the gas can and then the outboard motor. Carefully jumping into the bow of the dinghy I untied the painter and pushed off. We eased away calmly from Quest. The temperamental outboard finally throbbed to life. Halfway to the Customs dock I turned my head. Quest seemed to be in a world all by herself. The pirogues and small work boats crowding the anchorage bobbed gently at their moorings. Then there was Quest rolling and pulling at the mooring like a crazed tethered beast.

Wendy tied the dinghy off to a large iron ring after we pulled along side the government dock.

"Stay in the dinghy for a minute" I said.

"Why?"

"Take a look. If you haven't noticed there's no gate in that fence in front of you" I said pointing to the chain link and barbed wire fence which ran the entire width of the dock. I stood up in the dinghy and looked along the fence. "This is crazy. Where's the gate?" I asked Wendy.

"I don't see one either" she said.

That's when a young uniformed black man stepped from the Customs building and began to walk towards us up the dock. He stopped about halfway.

44

Rock and Roll

"Come on. The fence is open" he shouted.

"Where?" I shouted back.

He smiled and continued to walk towards the 'gate'. He pointed to the bottom right corner of one of the fence panels. "Pull the corner up. You can crawl through there" he said.

We jumped up on the dock and held the chain link fence up at the bottom.

"After you" I said to Wendy.

The Customs official strolled up and held his hand for me to shake. "Welcome to Statia."

"Thanks" I said. "What's with the fencing? Where's the gate?"

"Oh that. About a year ago Homeland Security told us we had to put a fence on the dock or they would black list the port. The fence came in a container. Someone forgot to order a gate. So there's our gate" he said pointing to the curled section of fence.

We walked with him back the short distance up the dock to the Customs building. Opening the door he gestured to chairs.

"Have a seat, be comfortable" he said.

Wendy handed him our passports.

"I bet I can guess who you two are" he said smiling and reaching for our passports.

"You can?" I said a bit surprised.

"Sure, I've kept an eye on your boat since I saw you come in this morning" he said. "I can't believe it took you this long to come to the dock" he said.

"Well, we had to clean up and square things away.

We've been sailing all night" I said in the way of an excuse.

"No, no, I don't mean that. I can't believe anybody could stay on a boat rolling that bad" he said letting out a great burst of laughter. "In another hour I was going to come out and see if you needed help."

Clearing Customs in the smaller Caribbean islands can be a very informal and friendly procedure. The officers at the government dock may see a few people a week. Most of the time they are glad to see a new face. After a cup of coffee, a pastry and an impromptu history lesson of Statia, we completed the procedures and left the Customs building with smiles on our faces and a plan to visit some of the sights that the officer had told us about. We turned left on Van Tonningenweg Road which runs north and south along the turquoise Oranjestad Bay waterfront. And there was Quest rocking to the rhythm of an unseen swell, tick tock.

We had walked only a hundred yards down the road when we heard a man call and wave from the veranda of an old building.

"Hello" he said as we stepped onto the veranda. He held out his hand. "Good morning. I am Gusta. You come to pay for the mooring ball" he said disappearing through the front door.

"Pay for the mooring ball? I completely forgot about it."

When he returned he asked "How many days will you be staying?"

I looked at Wendy. "One" we both said at the same time.

"Oh just one day" he said looking at both of us.

Rock and Roll

"That will be $20. You leave so soon" he said.

"Yes" I replied.

"Sorry about the harbor, it's a bit rough today. We've been watching your boat, very bad roll. If you don't mind me being nosy, how do you sleep on a boat that is rolling that bad?" he asked.

"We don't!" I said politely reaching for the receipt.

Retracing our steps to the road I looked at Wendy. "We've been watching your boat? Is that the royal 'we'?" I said.

"It's a small island. The 'we' is probably everybody on the island" Wendy laughed.

A bit down the road I noticed a sign for a scuba shop.

"Let's go in and see if they can tell us where a grocery store is" I said.

Looking through the open door I spotted a middle aged man dismantling a dive regulator on a workbench at the back of the shop. He noticed us and removed his glasses and wiped his brow with a rag.

"Come in, come in. You two must be the couple on the sailboat that came in this morning."

"We must be?" I said questioning.

"Yeah, George from Customs called me twenty minutes ago. Boy, we haven't seen a boat roll like that since the hurricane" he said. "Want to do a bit more diving this morning?" he asked.

"No thanks. But can you tell us if there's a grocery store in town?"

"Sure, just keep walking up the hill past the old fort.

You really should see the fort. When you're done there, keep walking on the same road till you get to the middle of town. Ask anybody there for the Chinese grocery store."

"Thanks" I said. "Are you American?" I asked.

"Yeah, came up from Miami five years ago. Came all the way in that power boat" he said proudly pointing to a v-hull in the anchorage. "Yeah, straight from Miami, non stop. I had drums of diesel lashed to the aft rail. I must have been crazy. It's a very good dive boat but it's a terrible ocean boat. I was seasick before I hit the Gulf Stream. Then the storms hit. What a mess. If I ever need another boat I'm going to have FedEx deliver it" he said laughing.

"Take it easy" I said leaving the shop.

We continued up the hill to Fort Oranje. Statia was first sighted by Columbus in 1493 but he made no attempt to land and plant the Spanish colors. Many years later, the island garnered the attention of the Dutch government. The Dutch West India Company seized a tremendous strategic advantage when they took possession of the island in 1636. They reported that the island was uninhabited on their first landing. The West India Company (WIC) were strictly importers and exporters. They had no designs to start plantations. Their plan was to turn Statia into the geographical center of the Dutch West India Company's holdings in the Caribbean. The plan proved to be a fantastic opportunity for WIC. They applied and were granted de facto jurisdiction over the island. The free port of Saint Eustatius was born.

A free port in the 1600's had a tremendous number of advantages over a taxed port. Merchant ships of all

nations were free to offload cargo and onload cargo
without the intervention of the taxman and the prying eye
of government. Pirates, villains and rogues were as
welcome as a British Rear Admiral. Enterprise of any sort
was the only reason for the existence of the Dutch West
India Company. Statia was a port where all were welcome
to trade in any cargo they wished. It wasn't a huge surprise
that Statia soon became one of the biggest transshipment
ports in the Caribbean. The vast majority of ships first
stopped in the free port of Statia before cargo was
reshipped and redistributed among the islands. Caribbean
cargo destined for Europe was routinely brought to Statia
before continuing onto Europe.

   With the large port filled with the morally good,
bad and ugly of all nations, it was logical that Statia would
become the crossroad of trade in contraband, slaves and
weapons. Law and order would have been difficult to
maintain in such a rough and tumble port. Who in their
right mind had any desire to police such a frontier?
Certainty not WIC or the Dutch Government. The job of
maintaining order was contracted to a loose band of
cutthroat pirates under the authority of WIC and the
Dutch government.

   In the late 1700's the fledgling United States of
America owed its survival to the Dutch West India
Company and their pirating friends. Statia played a vital and
mostly forgotten role in the American War of
Independence from Britain. It is agreed that more than half
of all munitions used by the Americans in the
Revolutionary War were supplied through Port Oranje on

Statia. It is widely believed that without the large quantity of arms flowing freely through the free port of Statia into the hands of American troops, the American revolution would have been a lost cause.

The British monarchy was extremely displeased with the Dutch West India Company and the Netherlands for profiteering on what they believed to be the wrong side of the war. In the closing years of the American revolution, the British declared war on Holland for supplying the Americans with arms. A fleet of fifteen ships was dispatched to Statia from the nearby island of St. Lucia in 1781. The fleet was commanded by George Bridges Rodney.

In the words of Admiral George Bridges Rodney "This rock, of only six miles in length and three in breadth, has done England more harm than all the arms of her most potent enemies, and alone supported the infamous rebellion... When I leave the island of St. Eustatius, it will be as barren a rock as the day it erupted from the sea. Instead of one of the greatest emporiums on earth, it will be a mere desert."

The British held onto their grudge for many years. Even years after the American revolution was won, the British still had it in for the tiny island of Statia. During a British Parliamentary debate, the ambassador Lord Stormont stated that "if St Eustatius had sunk into the sea three years before, the United Kingdom would have easily dealt with George Washington." Despite their bluster and gunboat diplomacy, the British navy did not turn Statia into a 'desert' nor did it 'sink the island'.

Rock and Roll

Statia is no longer a center of trade or one of the greatest emporiums on earth. It is a peaceful and beautiful island with an intriguing history that very few tourists ever get to enjoy. Today Fort Oranje has been meticulously restored and is very well maintained. Originally built from wood by the French in 1629, the current stone structure dates to British construction in 1703. The fort has seen its share of war and peace during its rich years of dominating Caribbean commerce.

The history of the Caribbean unfolded before our eyes as we stood on the recently reconstructed stone ramparts of Fort Oranje. A small herd of goats munched contentedly on tufts of grass growing between the stones in the parade ground. Looking down below the fort it was not difficult to imagine hundreds of sailing ships laying at anchor. The docks and warehouses brimmed with the wealth of the new world. Rich and poor, sailor and merchant mingled in crowded streets lined with pubs, stores and brothels. The rich merchants' houses and small garden plots dotted the hills behind the fort. Stone block walls along the waterfront that once protected Oranjestad from invaders and the ravishing forces of sea and hurricane stand sentinel to a bygone age. A short distance inland are the old walls of slave trading houses. There is nothing marking Statia's status as a hub for slaving in the Caribbean. These crumbling walls are the only monuments to the black men and women who made Statia a hub for slaving in the Caribbean.

It was not the British cannonade or even nature that eventually reduced Statia from the greatest free port in the

Caribbean to the sleepy place it is today. The end for Statia began with French occupation in 1775. The occupying French impressed onerous taxes on the Dutch merchants for the privilege of being 'protected' by the French military. This was the end of the free port of Statia. The taxes on goods flowing in and out of the port became a tremendous disincentive for anyone wishing to trade on the island. In a few years the trade in Oranjestad dropped to unsustainable levels. The island that once supported over 20,000 people is now home to only 3000. During the early 1800's the few remaining merchants who had traded on Statia for generations simply gave up and left. Statia suffered further decline when the lucrative Caribbean sugar cane industry was undercut by European sugar beet production. The final blow was the abolition of slavery. In 1816 the island returned to the hands of the Dutch where it has remained.

Like so many mighty ports down through history, Statia rose and set. At its zenith Oranje Bay accommodated over 3000 ships a year. Today only a handful of fishing pirogues dot its waters. What a change a few years can make to the fortunes of man. Statia's history as a world class trading port may be one of the most fascinating stories of the Caribbean that is seldom remembered outside of the Dutch islands.

Six

Rum and Noodles

It was very quiet at Fort Oranje, a normal day. Not a single tourist, tour guide or souvenir vendor entered the grounds. We had the fort to ourselves. Exploring this wonderfully preserved gem of history in the absence of distraction was a tonic for the imagination. Smiling at the young lady that kept watch over the entrance we walked the black basalt sidewalk to Fort Oranjestraat on our way to the town. The charming streets of the old city were as deserted as the parade grounds of the Fort.

"Excuse me ma'am" I said to a woman carrying a bag of groceries. "Can you tell me where the Chinese store is?" I said pointing to her bag.

"The Chinese store?" she repeated with a quizzical expression. "Oh, oh the grocery store" she said after thinking for a moment. "Keep walking this way and turn left on the third street. You won't get lost. Are you tourists?" she said with a pleasant smile.

"Not exactly tourists" I said.

"Oh" she said. "Are you the couple off the sailboat in the harbor?"

"Yes" I said.

Anticipating my surprise she looked at me and said "George mentioned it to me earlier this morning. Sorry about your boat rocking so hard. Sometimes the harbor can be bad for sailboats. Nice meeting you. I have to get my groceries home" she said smiling.

"Thanks for the directions" I said as she turned around to leave.

"You're very welcome" she said waving her hand.

We continued our stroll down Oranjestraat passing the ruins of the first synagogue on Statia. A couple of turns later we were standing in front of the store. I opened the door for Wendy. The pleasant aromas of coriander, lemon grass, cilantro and basil seemed to envelop us as we entered. What immediately caught my eye was a very old Chinese woman sitting on a stool in back with a large pot of simmering broth in front of her. Five toddlers stood waiting. Each youngster held a small bowl in front of their face.

"Wait till you see this" I said grabbing Wendy's arm and steering her to the back of the store. "Look, Grandma's cooking Ramen noodles."

"Great" Wendy said smiling.

I approached the inscrutable old Chinese lady and said "Ramen noodles."

"No rum, no rum, you want rum? She sell rum. Annie" she called to a middle-aged woman who was stocking a nearby shelf. "He want rum."

Grandma turned her attention to the noodles. Annie walked up to me and smiled.

"You want rum" she said.

Rum and Noodles

"No" I said shaking my head. "Ramen noodles" I repeated.

"Rum behind counter, noodles over there" she said very rapidly.

"NO, RA-MEN noodles" I said.

She looked back at me with a peevish look on her face and said "Rum and noodles? What rum and noodles?"

I stepped back in mild confusion mumbling words of acknowledgment. Trying to avoid Annie's continuing glare, I disappeared in aisle number one and immersed myself in the small selection of canned vegetables. I picked up a can of string beans from Serbia. How do you pronounce this? 'Boranija'. A second later I began to chuckle quietly. Then I began to laugh. Still laughing I found Wendy in the cookie aisle.

"Help me find the Ramen noodles."

She searched the aisles and came back in a moment.

"They're over here. How many do you want?" she asked.

"Just one."

I held the package up to Wendy's eyes.

"Rum and noodles" I said.

"Right, Ramen noodles" she said looking at me as if I had gone mad.

"No" I said. "Come over here."

I walked up to Annie at the counter. I held up the package of noodles with the front label showing.

"Ramen noodles" I said.

For a moment her face had a complete Asian blankness. Then she slapped my shoulder and burst out in paroxysms of laughter.

"Wuumman noodle" she said stretching out the O's in noodle. "Good joke. You funny man" she said continuing to laugh. She took the package and held it up. "Ma" she shouted to the back of the store. Grandma looked up from the pot and gave a shrug. "Wum and noodle" Annie shouted, chuckling. Grandma gave a second shrug and went back to her business. Annie now looked back at me expressionless. "You want? Five for one dollar."

"I'll take ten" I said.

"Best price on island, two dollar" she said.

"Do you have any money?" I asked Wendy.

It was approaching two o'clock. We had been awake for about thirty hours. Sleep deprivation on a cruising sailboat is neither unusual nor unexpected. On the other hand, the effects of sleep deprivation are usual and expected. Short term memory loss is the first sign. What day is it? What country are we in? While I waited for Wendy to pay for the several items on the counter I walked to the door and placed my hand on the door knob. I promptly fell asleep standing on my feet. I was jarred awake by someone coming through the door. Losing my balance I staggered back. The young man that was entering reached out and steadied me, placing his hand under my arm.

"Sorry for knocking into you. That was pretty clumsy of me" the man said releasing my arm.

"Quite all right" I said. "At least I wasn't having a good dream."

"I'm Albert" he said shaking my hand."

"Nice to meet you. This is my wife Wendy" I said.

56

Albert smiled and nodded. A moment later we heard the happy squeals of a gaggle of children.

"Uncle Albert" came the shouts from the back of the shop.

Within seconds we were surrounded by screaming happy children.

"Go back and eat your lunch" he said good spiritedly to the children.

They shuffled away in single file with their bowls.

"My sister's children" he said smiling and pointing to Annie. Annie smiled. "You must be the couple from the sailboat" he said.

"George call you this morning?" Wendy asked.

"No" he said. I opened the door to leave. "Hey, one second" he said. "I have a question. I was on the harbor road this morning. I own a restaurant in town. When I saw your boat..."

"Yes" I said.

"Well, I've always wondered how anybody could cook on a boat that's rolling around like that."

"I don't" I said smiling. "What kind of restaurant do you have?" I asked.

"Guess" he said with a glint in his eye.

"Chinese" I said.

"Close, it's Thai. I've got a real Indonesian Thai cook from Amsterdam. He's great. Why don't you come over for dinner later?"

"We don't eat out much. We're vegetarians" I said.

"Cool, my cook is vegetarian. We don't get too many grass and bark eaters here. I think it would make his

57

day to cook something without cow" he said laughing.

I looked at Wendy. She was smiling.

"Why not? I was planning on eating crackers tonight anyway" I said.

"Let me grab a couple things and I'll give you two a ride" he said.

Five minutes later we climbed into his minivan.

"Have you seen the fort?" he asked.

"Yes" I said.

"How about scuba diving?"

"I only scuba dive when I clean her bottom" I said. He looked curiously at Wendy. "No, when I clean Quest's bottom."

"Ah" he said smiling. "If you've seen the fort and you don't dive..." He shrugged his shoulders. "Well, that's about it." He pulled in front of the restaurant. "Come in and I'll introduce you to the cook. It's pretty quiet now. Jimmy's prepping for the dinner rush, if you can call it a rush. Here's a menu. Jimmy can make you anything. He's a genius."

"Rum and noodles?" I said.

"My sister told me about the rum and noodle thing. What a riot. They're going to be laughing about that for a month. Heeeere's Jimmy" he said as an older slight Asian man walked cautiously through the kitchen door. "I'll be right back" he said disappearing into the kitchen after saying something to Jimmy that we didn't understand.

"Vegetarian" Jimmy said.

"Yes, we've been vegetarian for thirty years."

Jimmy smiled politely and bowed.

"We don't get to talk to many vegetarian cooks" I said.

"Yes, vegetarian" he said nodding his head.

"We eat dairy products, but that's about it" Wendy said.

"Yes, vegetarian."

Albert reappeared from the kitchen.

"So have you two decided what you want?" he said walking to our table.

Jimmy bowed politely and scurried away through the double door of the kitchen.

"Hey I forgot to tell you. Jimmy doesn't speak a word of English. He was born in the Netherlands. He speaks Dutch Mandarin Indonesianese, can you believe it? Even my mother can't understand him." Wendy and I looked at each other and started to laugh compulsively. "Oh no" said Albert who started to laugh too.

"Right" I said. "The conversation was a bit one sided."

"Sorry about that. How about a beer while you wait?"

"A beer sounds good" I said.

"Heineken, Grolsch?" We thought about it for a second. "Hold on, I bet I know what you'd like. I just got twenty cases of Duvel off a tanker skipper yesterday. Duty free" he said winking.

"I could drink a Duvel" I said.

He hurried behind the bar and placed two Duvels and two glasses on a tray and walked over.

"Drink 'em slow. They're ten percent alcohol" he said cautiously.

"We'll be OK."

"Call me when you're ready" he said stepping back to the kitchen.

I poured Wendy's Duvel.

"Do you remember drinking Duvel when we were in Belgium?" I asked Wendy.

"I remember drinking the first Duvel. After that everything's a blank" she said.

I laughed. "That's about it. I remember waking up lying across the end of the bed with my clothes on the next morning" I said.

"Oh, that was you keeping my feet warm" she said smiling.

I took the first sip. It was ice cold, very malty, with a very alcoholic nose. I took another sip. The lack of sleep caught up with me almost immediately. My eyes began to close involuntarily. I started to feel very light headed and nodded off. I don't think I was out very long when I was awakened by the earthy sulfur smell of crude oil. 'Crude oil' I thought reaching over and touching Wendy on the shoulder. Her head bobbed up. Then we heard the low throaty rumble of a Texas accent.

"If you two wimps can't handle your booze, then pass it over to me."

I looked up to see a smallish weathered man in his forties wearing coveralls and an Exxon baseball cap. "What's your problem?" I asked.

"Drunk at 2 o'clock? If you were my crew I'd ship you home" he said.

"May I have the name of the person who just insulted my wife?" I said.

"What?" he said.

"What's your name Tex?" I said.

"Tex" he replied.

"OK. Let's try again. I'm David and this is Wendy."

"Nice to meet you David and Wendy" he said with a much less gruff tone. "I'm Jesse. You must be the couple off the sailboat in the harbor."

"What gave you that idea?" I said.

"I saw you this morning when you almost ran into me. I'm the captain of the Europa."

"Oil tanker?" I asked.

"All thousand feet of her."

"That explains the smell" I said.

"Ouch. With a mouth like that you could be a Texan."

"No, I'm a Canadian. We're a lot more obnoxious than Texans. Come join us."

He picked up his beer and sat down at our table.

"So what brings you to Statia?" Jesse asked.

"It's between Virgin Gorda and Nevis" I said.

"OK, that will do it" he said.

"And what brings you here?" I asked.

"I'm dropping off a couple million barrels of oil."

"Yeah, Wendy and I saw the tank on the hill when we sailed by this morning."

"You saw the tank? That's pretty funny. Then you

61

missed the other fifty tanks" he said.

"Fifty?"

"Yes, fifty. Statia's one of the largest terminalling facilities in the western hemisphere."

"Terminalling?" I asked.

"Yes terminalling, as in storage and blending" he said. "There are over 10 million barrels of petroleum over that hill" he said pointing north. "There's oil from ten different countries. I had breakfast this morning aboard a ship from the Jose terminal in Venezuela. Statia blends a big part of America's oil."

Albert walked over and set up a portable tray beside the table and brought out our meal.

"Jimmy made you his vegetarian favorites. This is basil eggplant and this is a pumpkin and tofu curry. I'll bring you some rice in a minute. What can I get you Captain?" he said to Jesse.

"Vegetarian favorites? Oh brother, I should have guessed. Just bring me another beer. Tofu puts me off my kibble."

We thoroughly enjoyed our meal and Jesse's lively accounts of life aboard oil supertankers. With full bellies, we paid the bill, thanked Albert for his hospitality and wished Jesse a safe voyage. Jesse stood up and shook my hand.

"Don't forget, we're only friends onshore. When we get out there" he said pointing to the ocean "out there, you're nothing more than a blow boater. So stay out of my way or I'll run you down" he said with a big laugh.

We retraced our way past the fort, the dive shop,

and the Parks building until we arrived back at the Customs dock. When we opened the door to Customs, George was leaning back in a chair completely absorbed in a three week old edition of the New York Times.

"Hello, hello" he said tipping forward in his chair. "Have a good lunch?"

"Best restaurant meal in two years" I said.

"Two years?"

"We don't get out much" Wendy added with a chuckle.

He checked our departure papers. "So you're off to Nevis. When are you leaving?"

"Probably tomorrow" I said.

"I've kept an eye on your boat. It doesn't look like the swell is any better. If that roll get too bad, come back and I'll let you sleep on my desk" he said.

"Thanks" I said opening the door.

"Wait a minute. I'll open the gate for you" he said.

The three of us walked down the short dock. George peeled back the corner of the chain-link fence and we slipped through. Dropping down from the dock we took our places in the dinghy.

George waved and said "Be safe."

We both waved back. I looked out in the bay. The swell was no better. Quest's mast was swaying from side to side with the consistent tempo of a metronome. Her rails were plunging with every roll.

"Jump on fast and be agile" I said pulling the dinghy alongside. Tying off the dinghy's painter I jumped aboard and gave the dinghy a shove away from Quest. "I'm not even going to try to pull her up on the davits today. We'll get her when we sail" I said.

We climbed into the cockpit and looked down into the cabin.

"Not too bad" I said grabbing onto the handholds and carefully lowering myself down the companionway.

I rolled onto the port settee and braced my feet against the mast. Wendy came below and slid onto the cabin sole, supporting her back against the settee and feet against the table base. After awhile, an uncomfortable silence fell over Quest.

Wendy was the first to speak. "So how do you think we should sleep tonight? There's no way I'll be able to sleep in the forward berth."

"I think our only choice is to lay on the floor and jam ourselves in with all the cushions we can find and hold on" I said.

An hour later I lay on my back, both feet pushing against a bulkhead, cushions on both sides propping me up and my hands and teeth clenched. Looking up through Quest's skylight into the cloudless night sky, the bright stars whipped dizzily from side to side.

Seven

Night and Day

Lying on the floor I watched the masthead light trace a line across the dark sky each time Quest snapped from side to side. She rolled to the port side and became motionless for a moment. Then in the snap of a finger the masthead swung to starboard arcing across the night sky at a dizzying speed. The stars were just streaks of light against a black background in the cabin skylight. By pressing my feet and head against bulkheads I found that I could at least retain the rhythm of the pitching floor. If only I could fall asleep and escape. The more I wished for sleep the more it eluded me. If only this roll would stop. I wished for just a moment of rest. I would have been happy with one skipped beat of the metronome. Thirty hours without sleep was having a very normal effect on my sense of well being. I watched the minutes click by on the clock at the nav table. At that moment I felt condemned to an endless sentence of enduring this unusually troublesome roll.

When the clock struck 12:00 midnight and the new day began I felt a renewed vigor. 'Why are you lying on the floor, fool?' I laughed to myself. 'Get up.' I carefully rolled over. Taking precaution to avoid crashing I crawled through the companionway into the cockpit. The moon had risen several hours earlier. Holding onto the cockpit combing I stared at the bright white full moon. The surface of the anchorage was completely placid. The mooring painters of the pirogues moored close to Quest hung loose at their bows. Quest's roll seemed so out of place. Heavy full keeled boats are a pleasure to sail. They are the strongest of any class of cruising boat. They won't win races but they are safe and easily sailed. The one disadvantage of heavy displacement deep keeled boats is that they roll significantly more at anchor than their shallower bulb keel brethren. Deep keeled boats are much more susceptible to the vagaries of underwater currents while anchored. Quest's tendency to roll at anchor was something that we learned to expect. No boat is perfect. Apart from her rollyness she was a good match for Wendy and me.

If there was ever a time to leave an anchorage, this was it.

"Wendy are you sleeping?" I called into the cabin.

"No" was her curt reply. "Time to go?" she asked.

"Get things ready in the cockpit. It is definitely time to go."

"I completely agree."

"Start the engine. I'm going forward to throw off the mooring. When the engine's running, turn everything on except the lights. I don't want to be blinded" I said.

A fresh steady breeze was blowing from shore. This would be a very quick and easy exit from Oranjestad Bay. It was no more complicated than pulling in the pendant and casting off. Holding the pendant in one hand I jammed a marlin spike into the overly tightened bowline knot that I had bent onto the pendant eye. A minute or two of fiddling with the knot and the seaweed and barnacle encrusted pendant was cast over.

"We're free. The wind is in our favor. Let her fall back on her own" I shouted from the bow.

Statia's anchorage is wide open. It is a good roadstead in favorable conditions. It can be a horrible anchorage in bad weather. Entering and leaving Oranjestad Bay is made extremely easy by its lack of complexity. I felt quite at ease to simply let the offshore wind do the job of pushing Quest out of port.

"Leave the engine in neutral unless we get close to something big."

As Quest slowly drifted away from the mooring Wendy said "We're going to come pretty close to that pirogue. Should I motor around it?"

"No" I said pulling a fender from the winch locker. I ran up on deck and held the fender alongside. Quest nudged up to the light pirogue and gently pushed it aside. "We should be good. It looks clear all the way out" I said unfurling the headsail.

With the headsail raised Quest responded smartly in the light air and pointed her bow seaward.

"That was a piece of cake" Wendy said.

When we were a quarter of a mile from land, Wendy put Quest in gear and spun her into the wind. The yankee luffed. The main was hauled up. It bellied and was cleated tight. When I pointed Quest south the bright moon light shone through the two billowing sails and illuminated the foredeck.

"Turn on the nav and deck lights and we'll figure out where we're going tonight" I said.

"What's our heading Captain?"

"140° true" I said re-checking the angle with the parallel rulers on the chart. "That should give us a pretty straight line to Pinney Beach on Nevis."

"Don't you want to stop in St Kitts?" Wendy asked.

"No. I think we should give St Kitts a pass. It's after midnight. If we get a good breeze we'll be in St. Kitts way too early. I'd rather get to Nevis in the early morning. If we arrive before dawn we'll heave to a mile off Pinney Beach" I said.

"OK" she replied. "I'll set the course for a straight run to Nevis. You know this course is going to bring us very close to the south shore of St. Kitts" she said looking at the line drawn on the chart.

"Yes, very close."

"Too close?"

"We'll see when we get there. It's just a little bit of incentive to keep our eyes open."

Without the least reservation I would describe Statia as one of the most peaceful islands in the Caribbean. With its lack of tourism and development, the inhabitants remain down to earth, honest and happy most of the time. Their long Dutch heritage gives them a practical outlook on life that is absent in many of the more popular islands. It was a wonderful place to visit. But with a roll that would make a fish vomit, and mooring for $20 dollars a day, it was also a good place to leave.

Night and Day

Quest sailed into the darkness. The silver light of the moon showed us our way. Quest's wake carved a straight line in the sea that stretched to infinity. In a night filled with moon, stars and cool tropical breezes, Quest settled into a spirited rhythm. A night sail on a benign ocean is a wondrous experience. The discomfort of the Statia roadstead seemed a lifetime away.

"Are you getting tired?" Wendy asked.

"I'm too exhausted to be tired" I said.

"Good. If you don't mind, I'm going to take a short siesta" she said.

Wendy stretched out on the cockpit cushions. Picking up the windbreaker lying across the cockpit table, I wrapped it around her shoulders. She wriggled into a comfortable position only after I turned off the overhead lights. I stood up and stretched my back and checked the instruments. Nothing could be better. We were gliding along at five knots under main and staysail. The cockpit fell silent. As Wendy nodded off the entire world seemed to fall asleep.

A moment later I went rigid when Wendy let out a blood curdling scream.

"There's something in the cockpit. Something big. It grabbed for my face then tried to bite my finger" she yelled. She jumped up on the bench waving at an imaginary object in front of her. "There it is!" she screamed pointing to the cockpit floor.

Sure enough, in the corner of the cockpit was a large flying fish.

"Turn the lights on" she said.

"Sure" I said flipping the switch and squatting down to take a closer look.

I pulled a towel from the winch locker and picked up the flying fish. It was about ten inches long. When I extended the wings they looked to be about twelve inches across. The back of the frightened fish was a deep blue with white stripes. The wings had a reddish tint edged with white and black dots. Its wings beat wildly as I raised it up.

"Want to take a look?" I said holding the fish up to Wendy.

"No way, throw it over. Get that thing out of my face" she said.

"It's just a fish. It's good luck when a flying fish hits you in the face."

"No it isn't. What's that, Greek mythology? It's only good luck when a fish hits you in the face."

I dropped it over the lee rail.

"You know, it wasn't so much the fish that bothered me. It was just the surprise. I was half asleep when it landed on me" she said.

"Why don't you lay down and go back to sleep?" I said.

"No thanks, I'm wide awake now" she said.

The staysail had been furled about an hour previously to slow our arrival time at Pinney Beach. We sailed at a slow steady four knots. The moon that lighted our way for much of our journey was beginning to set behind the mountains of St Kitts. The silhouette of the island and its towering 3800 foot dormant volcano etched a black jagged line across the starry night sky. On shore, the bright lights on the roads and highways created a zigzag pattern. The hillsides of St Kitts were only two miles away to windward. It looked so near. As we sailed even closer, I cautiously switched off the autopilot. Approaching an unfamiliar island in darkness can be unsettling. Perspective is distorted at night. The shore always appears closer than it does during the day. Fear of grounding is exaggerated in your mind. After disengaging the autopilot I took the wheel and set the depth sounder alarm to one hundred feet. The chart clearly indicated that the contour lines ran in smooth parallels from shore.

"We'll stay out of trouble if we keep between the fifty and one hundred foot contour" I said pointing to the chart.

We sailed a course closer to shore until the depth alarm sounded. At a quarter of a mile from the beach, the small white houses scattered on the hillside seemed to jump out of the darkness.

"I think that this is plenty close" I said nudging Quest's helm further away from the breakers on the shore line.

"I was wondering when you'd turn off. The shore looks so close" Wendy said.

We still had a very favorable wind. We sailed back and forth within our contour range. The good wind that we had experienced during the night couldn't last much longer. It was just a matter of time before we fell into the lee of the towering Mt. Liamuiga on our port side. Several more miles down the coast the wind dropped suddenly to eight knots. The sea was as smooth as a pond. It reflected the bright stars like a mirror.

"We need to catch a bit more air" I said getting up and unfurling the jib and the staysail.

The sails filled. Quest surged forward and heeled modestly. I glanced to the east. The purples and dark violets of false dawn drew a faint line across the distant horizon. The sun would soon be with us. '♫ Day and night, night and day.' This would be our second sunrise without sleep in fifty hours. The time between the first appearance of the false dawn and sunrise always seems to drain me of energy. This morning my spirits were buoyed by the first sight of Nevis only a few miles away. I stood up at the wheel. The island of Nevis is small and almost perfectly round with a single potentially active volcano at its center. On its north slope, the lush greenery rises from the water's edge to a height of over 2300 feet. The volcano dominates the landscape and gives the island a distinctly tropical appearance.

"How about a cup of tea?" Wendy offered.

"Caffeinated Earl Grey" I said.

"No herbal tea this morning?" she said smiling.

"No, I think I need to wake up a bit. I can't keep my eyes open."

Wendy disappeared into the cabin and returned ten minutes later with two cups of tea. "Here you go" she said handing a mug up the companionway.

"Thanks honey. I can use this" I said.

We sat beside each other on the starboard cushions. The cloudless eastern sky exploded with brilliant color as the first golden orange rays of the sun pierced the darkness. The mist shrouding the top of Mt. Nevis caught the first rays of the morning sun to create an ethereal golden halo around its summit.

Once past Basseterre Bay on the southern tip of St. Kitts we came out of the island's lee. The wind and sea increased dramatically as we sailed across the two mile channel separating the islands. In minutes we were out of the seaway and sailing smoothly along the southern shore of Nevis. As we pressed closer to our destination, the rising sun slowly illuminated the steep sides of the volcano giving us our first view of the rich tropical vegetation that extends from the waterline to its top. Sailing along the palm fringed coastline was a perfect picture of a tropical paradise.

"This is unbelievable" Wendy said. "Sandy beaches, palm trees. The mountain makes the island look like it could be in the south Pacific."

I started the engine when we approached the northern end of Pinney Beach. I went forward to lower the main while Wendy furled the jib. Pinney Beach stretched for miles. We motored a course about a thousand feet from the beautiful sandy shore until we arrived opposite the anchorage.

"OK, bring us in close and let me know when we have twenty feet."

Waiting at the bow I slipped the handle onto the windlass break.

"Fifteen feet" Wendy yelled.

I dropped the anchor in crystal clear blue water over a powdery white sand bottom. Wendy reversed the engine and the anchor set immediately.

"That was probably the easiest anchoring ever" I said when I returned to the cockpit.

"This is going to be a great stop" Wendy said.

Quest was well anchored in paradise. A mild offshore breeze kept us cool and kept Quest's bow pointed to the volcano.

"Do you know what the best part of Nevis is?" I asked Wendy.

She shrugged.

"There's absolutely no roll."

"You're right. This is as smooth as being on the hard" she said.

I covered the mainsail while Wendy stowed the gear.

"I'm going to sleep for about twenty-four hours" I said while I was coiling the furling line.

"I don't think we've had a nicer anchorage in months" Wendy added.

After one more check on the anchor I was starting down the cockpit ladder when we heard a dinghy approaching at high speed. A cruiser in a bathing suit and tank top nudged his dinghy alongside Quest and cut his engine.

"How it's going?" I said.

"Terrible. It just doesn't get any worse."

The last thing I needed right now was a conversation with an upset cruiser. "Great. I mean, sorry. Have a nice day" I said smiling and turning away.

"Hold on. Wait. There's something I have to tell you. You haven't checked in yet, have you?"

"No, we just got here a half hour ago."

"If you know what's good for you, you'll just pick up and leave. The police here are crazy. They threw me in jail for the night. When I went to check in to Customs yesterday, the police came out and searched my boat" he said pointing to a grimy catamaran anchored beside Quest. "They brought the dogs!"

"Yeah. So what?" I said impatiently.

"So what! They found one lousy joint in a locker. They deported me. Look at my passport. It's stamped 'Undesirable' " he said holding it up. "Now everybody's going to want to search my boat."

"Sounds right" I said disappearing into the cabin.

As we listened to him curse and yell on his way back to his boat Wendy looked out the porthole and asked "What's up with that guy?"

"Nothing, he's just feeling a big unloved today" I said.

Eight

Down on Main Street

It was 9 o'clock in the morning and about two days past my bedtime. I took one last look at the incredibly beautiful sun-drenched Nevis volcano as I eased down the companionway. The image of this perfect tropical paradise lingered on my sleep-deprived retinas as I lay down on the forward berth and pulled the sheet over my head. The events of the previous days seemed to play and replay in my racing mind as I tossed and turned trying to shake off wakefulness. I soon relaxed and felt the tension draining from my body. 'This is more like it' I said to myself fading into sleep. In what felt like a moment I heard the banging of a pot hitting the burner on the galley stove.

"Go to bed Wendy" I said abruptly.

I received no reply. The sound of the pot being dropped on the stove burner for a second time was followed by Wendy clearing her throat.

"Do you have to make so much noise?" I said getting up to retrieve a set of earplugs from the dresser drawer.

I looked out the starboard portlight. The rising morning sun was was in just about the same position as when I had laid down. It was going to be harder to get to sleep than I had imagined. I lay down once again and placed the pillow over my eyes. A second later I felt Wendy shaking my shoulder.

"Wake up, wake up, I made some tea for you" she said.

"I don't need any tea. I need to get some sleep" I said.

"How long are going to sleep?" she asked.

"I don't know how long I'm going to sleep. Just keep the noise down" I said gruffly.

I rolled over with my face to the bulkhead. Again I felt Wendy's hand on my shoulder. This was getting annoying.

"How much longer are you going to sleep?" she asked again.

I turned over and pulled the earplug out of my right ear. "As long as I can" I said.

"Don't you think that twenty-two hours is enough?" she asked.

"Sounds good to me" I said. "Yeah. Wake me in twenty-two hours."

"OK, then wake up" she said smiling. "You've been asleep since yesterday."

"It's Thursday?" I said.

"Yeah it's Thursday. Just sit up and I'll bring you a cup of tea" she said. "It's nice to see you back with the living. I thought you went into a coma" she said laughing as she handed me the tea.

"I've been asleep for a day?"

"Almost a day" she said. "Any good dreams?"

"No dreams that I remember" I said. "Oh no, Immigration. I almost forgot. We're overdue for Immigration."

I bolted straight up in the berth. I was wide awake now.

"I don't think they care if we're a little late" Wendy said.

"This isn't a little late" I said. "Remember the dope dude that came up to Quest yesterday morning?"

"Yeah."

"He told me that the police brought the dogs to his boat because he was late checking in. We better get moving. Put on some nicer clothes. Let's go."

We piled into the dinghy. After a quick trip to the bow to check on the ground tackle and snubber I turned the dinghy and raced from Pinney beach to the Charlestown ferry pier. Wendy secured the dinghy to the dock.

"Well, where's Immigration?" I said looking around for a government building.

"There is no Immigration. I tried to tell you in the dinghy. Now I know you weren't paying attention. We have to check in at the police station" Wendy said.

"Well, where is it?" I said impatiently.

"Let me check" she said opening the fold-out map in the cruising guide. "Here it is. It's on Main Street. We go south on Low Street for a hundred yards then turn right onto Main Street. Then down Main Street for about a quarter mile."

Down on Main Street

I was still a bit groggy. The old colonial buildings were a blur. My heart pounded and I sweated in the tropical heat as we hurried down Main Street.

"There it is" Wendy yelled from a few feet behind me. "It's over there on the left."

After opening the front door of the police station we passed into the lobby. The duty officer sat behind an old, dark wooden counter with a new glass partition resting on top.

"I'm here" I said to the officer a bit breathless.

The officer nonchalantly turned his head. My t-shirt was drenched from perspiration and I was panting like a dog.

"You OK?" the officer asked. "You look like you're having a heart attack."

"I'm fine" I said.

"Sit down over there and take a few deep breaths. I'll be with you in a couple of minutes" he said.

Wendy and I took our places on a bare wooden bench between a young mother and her nine year old daughter on our right. An inebriated, unshaven disheveled man in his thirties was sitting on our left. Judging from the sour looks and the comments exchanged by the two adults on each side of us, we gathered we were temporarily providing a DMZ zone between a couple with a serious family problem.

The officer got up from his desk and walked to the glass partition. "Get over here Jimmy" the officer shouted to the scruffy man beside me.

The man slowly got to his feet and staggered to the window. Weaving from side to side he looked bleary eyed at the officer.

"Drunk again Jimmy" the officer said with a low authoritative growl. Jimmy looked down and didn't say a word. "OK Louisa, take the child and go to your Nana's and stay there! Jimmy, you go home. If you mess up again I'll lock you up for sure. Do you understand? Now get out of here and behave yourself!"

Jimmy muttered incoherently and shuffled out of the lobby.

"Louisa" the officer said quietly when Jimmy had cleared out of the lobby. "Hold on. Go through there" he said pointing to an oak paneled door. "I'll have Nathan run you over to your Nana's. Stay away from your house for now. That's all I can do. If he does it again, I'll lock him up."

"Thanks" she said passing through the door.

The officer looked in our direction. "So what's your problem?" he growled in our direction.

"You're in trouble now, Wendy" I whispered out of the side of my mouth. "Just smile and let me do the talking."

"What, what? Speak up. I didn't hear you" the policeman said.

I got up and walked to the window. "Hi, we're from the sailboat off Pinney Beach" I said smiling.

"You again. Didn't I deport you yesterday? You have the nerve to come back?" he said standing up and unlocking the door. "Get in here" he ordered.

Down on Main Street

We passed through the narrow entrance into the office.

"You're done for now. I catch you with marijuana and deport you and you haven't got the brains to leave? Do you think I'm stupid?" he shouted.

"No, you don't look stupid. Do we really all look the same?" I said in a strong voice.

He stepped back. Every bit of expression drained from his face.

"Sorry" I said. "I didn't really mean that. What I meant to say was, we aren't the dopers off the catamaran. We're just another white couple with similar t-shirts."

A tiny smile slowly formed in the corners of his mouth. Then his entire face began to beam. "No" he laughed. "It's me that should be sorry. You don't all look the same, just very similar. Especially when I only take a quick look. Please have a seat" he said looking in Wendy's direction. "Allow me" he said pulling a chair a short distance across the office for Wendy.

He held the chair out for Wendy while she seated herself. Wendy looked at me, smiled and raised her eyebrows.

"You can get your own chair. Over there" he said pointing to the corner.

I picked the chair up and placed it softly beside Wendy.

"So you wish to check in. Your passport and boat papers, please." Wendy unzipped her knapsack and presented the documents. "

Are you the Captain?" he said to Wendy.

"No. He's the Captain" she said pointing to me.

"Well Captain, you checked out of Statia two days ago. It took you forty hours to sail thirty miles? That must be some sort of record."

"Not for me. We arrived yesterday morning" I said.

"And you waited a day before you checked in? How long have you been in the Caribbean? You know that you should be prompt when presenting yourself to Immigration" he said. He stood up and picked up a ringing telephone. "So maybe there's some reason why you didn't want to check in yesterday?" he said holding the phone's receiver in his right hand.

He turned away from Wendy and me to take the call. "Hello. Police station. OK, OK, I'll send some one out right away. Stay where you are" he said into the receiver. He placed the receiver back into the cradle. Turning back he seemed to be lost in thought for a moment. "That was Louisa" he said absentmindedly. "Jimmy passed out dead drunk right in front of the police station. Wait a minute. I have to get an officer to drag him onto the sidewalk." He opened a door and yelled down a corridor. "Someone go get Jimmy and pull him onto the sidewalk."

An echoing voice from another room said "Yes, right away Sergeant."

"So why exactly did it take you so long to check in?" he asked again.

"Well" I started. "Three days ago we were in Virgin Gorda. You know in the British Virgins. When we got to Saba we couldn't find the moorings so ..."

"Wait a minute, wait a minute. I don't care about Virgin Gorda. Oh forget it. Do you have any contraband?"

"No contraband" I said.

"That includes drugs. Do you have any drugs?"

"No drugs" I said.

He pulled our passports across the desk and inked the stamp. Thump thump, both passports were stamped, dated and pushed back to Wendy.

"You're anchored off Pinney Beach? If you move your boat to another anchorage, you must come back and tell us. Do you understand?" he said.

"Yes" I said.

"You can go. Stay out of trouble" he said pointing to the door.

He pressed a button under the desk and unlocked the door. Wendy and I left the police building and stood on the steps under the shade of a banyan tree.

"Well that was a bit different" Wendy said.

"It's the first time we've had to check in at a police station. He wasn't quite as laid back as the average Immigration officer. Then again Immigration officers aren't usually wrangling drunks" I said laughing. "Oh brother. Look up the street."

"What?" Wendy said.

"Over there on the right side of the street" I said pointing. Jimmy was laying on his side sleeping under a tree.

"At least they gave him some shade" Wendy said.

"How about we just go back to Quest and take it easy? Maybe polish some stainless" I said.

"OK" Wendy agreed.

Quest in the Caribbean

We retraced our path back down Main Street. When we turned onto Low street we had a straight view of the government dock.

"Look. The ferry to St. Kitts is at the wharf. Do you want to take a boat ride instead?" I said.

"Definitely. That sounds a lot more fun than polishing stainless."

Wendy tightened the cinches of her small backpack as we raced down the street and asked a dock idler where we could find the ticket office for the ferry. The man stood up, laughed and pointed to a three foot sign over our heads 'St. Kitts Ferry'.

"Two return tickets for St. Kitts" I said to the young lady behind the counter.

She took our dollars and slid two tickets through the hole in the glass partition. As we walked the short distance to the ferry another young lady waved both arms frantically motioning us to get on board.

"Hurry hurry" she said "Da ferry leaving. Get on! Get on!"

We hurried and jumped onto the half empty ferry and stood waiting for fifteen minutes with a half dozen happy grinning tourists. Before the Captain even started the engines a mildly sunburned woman in her mid forties turned to Wendy and me.

"I'm Nancy" she said. "Are you here with the 'Change of Latitudes Tour'?" she asked.

"Change of Latitudes?" I asked.

"You know 'Change of Latitudes'" she repeated.

At that moment there was some doubt in my mind

whether Wendy and I had taken the right ferry. "I think this is the ferry to St. Kitts" I said to her.

"Oh yes, isn't Nevis just grand?" she said.

"Sure, Nevis is terrific" Wendy said.

Wendy was smiling, nodding her head. I could just feel her trying to anticipate the woman's next remark.

"This is the ferry to St. Kitts?" I asked her.

"Oh yes, St. Kitts" she said nodding and smiling. "We all flew down from Baltimore two days ago. That's my husband there leaning over the bow. He gets sea sick very easy" she whispered in a conspiratorial tone.

Apparently her husband was expecting rough seas. The dock lines were still well secured and he was already looking a bit green.

"So what's this 'Change of Latitudes tour?'" Wendy asked.

"Oh you haven't heard about it. It's a great program. The First Secretary of St. Kitts and Nevis gave our club a presentation on 'The Program' this spring." She let the suspense build for a moment. "The government of St. Kitts and Nevis is offering citizenship to a select group of American citizens. Within three months my husband Harold and I will have full citizenship in this wonderful country" she said as the dock lines were thrown off.

The dock hands gave the ferry a great shove and the Captain gunned the engines. Nancy temporarily lost her footing and crashed into my shoulder.

"We're not boat people" she said apologetically.

I looked at the bow. Harold had both hands on the bow railing with his head pointed straight down. When the ferry came opposite Pinney Beach I pointed out Quest to Nancy.

"There's our boat" I said.

"That's nice" she said politely. "Harold and I have been selected for the Citizenship Program. Many of our friends are on the boat too" she said nodding. "In three months we'll all have full citizenship in St. Kitts and Nevis."

"Both islands?" I said joking.

"Oh yes. St. Kitts and Nevis are one country you know."

"Right" I said.

"The best thing of all is that our real estate agent in Nevis took care of the whole process."

"You mean your lawyer?" I asked

"No, that's how great the program is. We bought a villa just outside Charlestown on Nevis and our realtor took care of all the paperwork for citizenship."

"But you're an American" I said. "Why do you want citizenship in St. Kitts and Nevis?"

"That's the fantastic thing about the program. All we had to do was buy a villa for $750,000 and they gave us the citizenship free. Isn't that great?" she said first looking to me then to Wendy.

"Congratulations" Wendy said with a smile.

"We're so happy with our new villa. We saw it for the first time this morning. Of course the realtor sent us scads of photos before we signed the contract. It's just beautiful. You'll have to come up and see us. I better go see if Harold is OK. Bye bye" she said waving and disappearing through the door onto the forward deck.

Down on Main Street

"She sounds pretty happy with her new purchase" I said.

"I'll say. I bet that Nancy and Harold are going to fit in great in St. Kitts and Nevis" Wendy commented.

"This program sounds like a pretty good deal. We should get in on it" I said.

"Right" Wendy said as the ferry tied off to the pier.

We spent a few hours walking about the old colonial town of Basseterre. The business district of Basseterre is devoted to catering to the shopping needs of the cruise ship passenger. There are plenty of Authentic Diamond and Colombian Emerald Stores for everyone. St. Kitts has much to offer, including $750,000 free citizenship.

Nine

Half a Volcano

Checking in at the Nevis police station and taking the ferry to St. Kitts was about as much fun as we could take that day. After we arrived back at the Charlestown dock we immediately jumped into the dinghy, sped back to Quest and laid down for an extra long nap. It was quite a luxury to feel secure in the knowledge that we wouldn't be rolled out of our berth. The mild ocean wave that gently curled onto Pinney Beach was soothing and soporific. The calmness of the Nevis anchorage and the beauty of the landscape was a very enjoyable gift.

After another twelve hours of sleep, I woke refreshed and ready to explore our new found paradise. Sitting in the cockpit with a cup of tea in my hand I couldn't imagine a more beautiful place to be. It was picture perfect.

The white pristine sand of Pinney Beach stretches for miles. The coastline is dotted with an unbroken green line of palm trees. The volcano which seems bejeweled by green tropical vegetation rises gently from the aquamarine coastline. Halfway to the summit it curves precipitously upwards and disappears into the mist and cloud. The island has a classic volcanic profile that inspires the imagination and invokes thoughts of the South Pacific. It was a perfect day to take a stroll on the perfect island.

I pulled the dinghy up to the boarding ladder. We eagerly jumped in, excited to see the island from land. We had no particular plans as we motored to the Charlestown pier. The hot tropical sun was still low on the horizon. The morning dew dripped from the old tires that were strung along the concrete municipal dock as fenders. It was early. The city of Charlestown was barely awake. A small group of fishermen were returning in their pirogues from a night on the ocean. The hustle and bustle of a normal weekday was still an hour away.

Crossing the dock and walking a short distance south we came to the Charlestown vegetable market. Sitting on two abandoned crates we watched the vendors busily unload trucks loaded with yams, avocados, grapefruit, oranges, breadfruit, tomatoes, pumpkins, salad greens, potatoes and even seagrapes. Under the persuasive instruction of a local policeman the trucks were quickly emptied. The tables in the pavilion were stacked to capacity. The vegetable stall ladies took their respective places on stools beside their tables. As if cued the ladies started fanning their faces with one hand and waving flies away from the produce with the other.

"How much for your tomatoes?" I asked the lady in the first stall.

"My tomatoes?" she said meeting my eyes. "Oh dees, dees the good tomatoes. They four dollar a pound."

She reached over her pile of big tomatoes and picked one up.

"No thanks" I said.

We pressed on and asked the price of tomatoes at the next stall. The second lady took a quick glance at the lady in the first stall.

"Four dollar. But my tomato better than her tomato" she said.

The first lady threw up her hands, let out a few angry breaths of air and replied with disdain "Her tomato from St. Kitts. St Kitts tomato no good."

As we walked further into the market the two ladies kept up a constant bickering banter.

When we were out of earshot, Wendy turned to me. "Four dollars a pound?" she said.

"That's what I heard. Hey, it's eight in the morning. We'll come back at 11:00. I bet the price of tomatoes will come down in a couple of hours, especially when they have to reload the truck" I said.

Our mission for that day was to explore the wonderful island of Nevis. We continued our stroll up Low Street until it intersected with Main Street. The downtown area of Nevis is a charming mix of old colonial and modern architecture that blends nicely to maintain a balance between new and old. Many of the interiors of the very old buildings have been modernized to accommodate the needs of 21st century businesses. The central business area is small and easily covered by foot in less than a half hour.

"Well, that sure didn't take long" Wendy said when we had made our third pass up and down Main Street. "Now where do you want to go? Someplace exciting?

Maybe the library?" she laughed.

"We'll go to the library later. I have an idea. There's a local bus terminal here" I said pointing to the map of Nevis. "Why don't we take a poor man's tour of the island? I bet the buses are only a couple of bucks. The terminal is a little past the police station on the left."

Main Street was just beginning to fill up with early morning shoppers.

"There it is" I said as we continued up the street and turned the corner.

Wendy and I walked up to the first minibus in a paved lot with about thirty vans of various makes and models. Each bus had a similar capacity of about 15 passengers.

"Excuse me" I said speaking through the driver's window. "We'd like to take a bus around the island."

"Charter. Yes Mon" he said straightening himself in the seat.

"Hold on. We don't want to charter. We just want to stay on your bus and go around the island and come back to this terminal."

"Bus don't go round the island" he said slouching back into the seat and pulling his cap over his eyes.

"Thanks" I said.

We walked up to another minivan. This time I tried to make myself better understood.

"Good morning" I said. "I would like to buy a ticket, a round trip ticket around the island and come back to the terminal."

"Bus don't go round island" the driver said.

I looked at our map of Nevis. There was definitely a paved road all the way around Nevis.

"What's going on?" I said to Wendy. "I'm going to ask that policeman over there." I walked to the edge of the hardtop where the policeman was standing in the shade of a tree. "Excuse me sir" I said.

"Yes?" he said politely.

"I've asked a couple of drivers if my wife and I could pay for a return ticket around the island. They refused."

"Yes, oh course" he said matter-of-factly.

"Well, why won't they take us?" I said.

"The buses don't go around the island. They only go half way around the island. They start here. They either go north or they go south. When they get half way around the other side of the island they turn around. Buses never go all the way around the island, never."

"Why?"

"I don't know. Ask them. That's bus drivers for you" he said laughing.

I walked up to the first driver to whom we had spoken. "We want to go north towards the airport, stay on your bus, and when you are at the end of your route on the other side of the island, we want to stay on the bus and come back with you. We'll pay you for a return ticket."

"Sure, so that's what you want to do. You should have said that the first time" he said.

I paid him and he handed back the change.

"You sit up here. Right behind me" he said pointing. "I give you real good tour of Nevis. My name Jacob."

I introduced Wendy and myself. "When does the bus leave?"

"When full" he said nodding his head and smiling.

We climbed on board. Within fifteen minutes every seat on the bus was filled. He started the engine, leaned over and gave us a complete breakdown of the passenger manifest.

"Almost everybody going to jobs at resort. Dem tree, dey going to airport. The old lady, she's Annie. She going to babysit for daughter in Mt Lily."

"Do you know everybody?"

He looked over his shoulder. "Yeah" he said.

The clean and ornately painted minibus left the terminal. We proceeded up Main Street and passed through the commercial district. Within a half mile we were well out in the countryside and approaching the resort on Pinney Beach. Half the passengers rose to their feet as the bus slowed in the parking lot. Jacob said good morning to each disembarking person.

"Dat most of em" he said to me as he turned onto the highway. "Just two more stops."

The portion of the coastal highway that connects the city of Charlestown to the airport on the northern tip of the island is a delight for the eyes. The aquamarine shallows that surround the island blend to an infinite Caribbean blue. In the distance we could make out the island of St. Kitts to the north. The air was crystal clear. As we drove further into the foothills the volcano loomed over us.

"Have you ever walked to the top of the volcano Jacob?"

"Dat some walk up to volcano, real big walk. Take all day. I too old. I sixty-five" he said proudly. "I walk up everyday when I fifteen. Top of hill lot further now."

The coastal road wound further north. Half the time we were surrounded by tropical vegetation and foothills then we would descend gentle inclines to pass along pristine white sand beaches. Reaching the north corner of the island, Jacob touched me on the knee and pointed ahead to the airport.

"Runway too short. In maybe two years they make runway longer. Then we get more tourists" he said.

Jacob pulled the bus in front of the airport terminal. He exchanged pleasantries with the passengers and closed the door. Before he put the bus back in gear, he turned his head and spoke to the old lady in the rear seat of the bus.

"Miss Annie, you come and sit up here" he invited. Annie began to get to her feet.

Jacob ran to the back of the bus and gently helped her up the aisle to the front seat next to us.

"Dis my friend Annie" he said to Wendy and me.

I took the frail woman's hand in mine and gave it a light squeeze. She smiled and nodded without saying a word.

"Dey not tourists" Jacob said. "They own sailboat."

I looked at Jacob. "I didn't tell you that we were cruisers" I said.

"Are you?" he said.

"Yes" I said.

"See" he said.

"How did you know?" Wendy asked.

"Dat easy" he said. "I hear you talking about your boat when we passed Pinney. Your boat, Quest."

"Yes" I said.

"And tourists don't have tans like that" he said pressing his finger gently into my forearm. He looked at Annie. "We drop Annie off now."

Annie looked over and smiled a toothless grin at Wendy and me. "Daughter live on Mt Lily, just up there" she said softly to us as the bus labored up the steep grade.

Jacob pulled in front of a simple white and pink cottage on the hillside. He opened the door and helped Annie down the steps of the bus.

"I pick you up at 5:00?" he said.

"Yes" she said smiling then walked slowly towards the house.

The bus was now empty except for Wendy, Jacob and me.

"Now we have some fun?" he asked.

"Fun sounds good" I agreed.

"We go to Brick Klin."

"They make bricks on Nevis?" I asked.

"No, not kiln, no bricks. Brick Klin is name of small village on windy side where my friend live" he said.

We drove around to the dryer east side of the island. Herds of cattle grazed short grass on gently sloping rocky terrain.

"Dis Brick Klin" Jacob announced as he drove up a side street.

A row of small concrete houses painted in pink, green and blue pastels were packed tightly along one side of the narrow street.

"This is very nice" I said politely.

"No, dis not it. Just wait. I tink you never seen dis before."

He pulled the bus in front of one of the houses.

"Now we wait" he said opening a cooler beside him and pulling out three soft drinks.

"What are we waiting for?" Wendy asked.

"Just wait. Won't be long."

In about ten minutes a young man left the front door of the house, got into a car on the driveway and sped down the hill. When he pulled opposite the bus he honked his horn. Jacob waved with two fingers.

"Now we wait again."

Another ten minutes passed. Jacob sat bolt upright in the seat.

"Over dere. Look, look. Dey coming out of da bush" he said pointing at a thicket beside a house.

I looked again. At first one monkey came into view, then another four.

"They bad green monkey" he said.

"Bad?" I said.

"Yes bad. Look" he said.

Half a Volcano

The two foot tall monkeys acted very suspiciously as they entered the carport of his friend's house. The lead monkey grabbed the garbage bin by the handle. Dragging it to the driveway, he knocked it over, spilling the contents everywhere.

"Bad!" Jacob yelled jumping out the door and running towards the house.

The troop spotted Jacob and scattered. The leader turned, stood up on his hind legs, raised his arms and screamed intimidatingly as Jacob approached. Jacob picked up a branch and went after the leader. The monkey dropped to the ground and took off like a shot. Jacob returned to the bus and climbed in laughing all the way.

"Dey really bad monkeys. Every time my friend leave for work the monkeys come and do mischief. They break window. One time dey got into house and stole hi-fi, kitchen knife and bottle of rum. I wouldn't want to be around when dey party and drunk on rum with knives" he said pushing in the clutch.

We rolled down the hill laughing.

"We pick up passengers for Charlestown now" he said.

We drove further down the coast road until we reached a settlement called Butler.

"We turn around and go back now."

"Why don't the buses go all the way around the island?" I asked.

"Can't" he replied. "Two different companies. We drive here. Dey drive dere. Dat deir area" he said pointing further up the road.

He seemed in quite a hurry as we raced back towards Charlestown.

"Not many passengers" Jacob said absentmindedly.

"There's three" Wendy said pointing to two women and an old man standing on the shoulder.

"We in for trouble now. Dis guy very angry man" Jacob said pulling up to the corner.

The women boarded the bus and took seats beside Wendy and me. The old man stood on the shoulder and stared into the bus.

"You come now?" Jacob said patiently.

The old man turned his head and spit on the shoulder of the road. Jacob closed the door, leaving the man in a cloud of dust as he sped off.

"What was that all about?" I asked.

"We have history" Jacob said with a shrug.

We passed the airport following the same stretch of road that we had traveled earlier. At the top of the island Jacob turned south along the green coast of Nevis.

"You want some vegetables?" he asked.

"Sure" I said.

"My friend have garden stand. We get vegetables."

Just past the Pinney resort Jacob turned into a driveway and turned off the engine. Wendy and I got out and walked to the stand and picked out two pounds of the best tomatoes that we had seen in months, a cucumber and some lettuce.

"That be two dollars" the vendor said.

Climbing onto the bus I held up the bag and said to Jacob "Two dollars."

"He charge you right price. You don't get dat price in Charlestown" he said.

"You're right" I said.

"I drop you off at pier" he said turning down Low Street. "Have a good tour?" he asked.

"Excellent" I said.

"You like Nevis?" he asked.

"I think Nevis is great" I said shaking his hand.

"How did the monkeys get to Nevis?" Wendy asked while getting off the bus.

"They sailed their monkey boats here" he said winking. "Most people say British sailors brought dem hundred years ago" he said.

We waved as he turned his bus around and headed back into Charlestown.

Ten

Island on Fire

Nevis is a visually stunning island. The people that call the island their home are among the most friendly that we had seen anywhere in the world. We could have stayed on Nevis for a very long time if it were not for the inevitability of a chance encounter with a big bad hurricane.

A few days after our arrival in Nevis we continued our slow sail towards 12° south latitude. This would put us on the south coast of Grenada where it was agreed that we would be safe from hurricanes. The next stop on our Caribbean itinerary was Little Bay on the island of Montserrat. The weather fax from the previous day indicated that an unusually strong tropical wave would pass through the Caribbean. Despite the natural beauty and our attachment to Nevis, it was time to move on and take advantage of a short period of moderate to good sailing conditions.

The Lesser Antilles is an archipelago of islands that form the southwestern boundary of the Caribbean. This tightly arranged group of volcanic islands stretch from Saba in the north all the way to the island of Trinidad. Many of the islands that make up the Lesser Antilles are dominated by active volcanoes that pose major threat to life. Mariners traveling along these fiery islands will find good shelter from North Atlantic storms as well as line of sight navigation. Even the greenest rookie would find it difficult to get lost in the Lesser Antilles. We had found our sweet spot. Each island in the chain can be seen by its neighbors and they are no more than a short day sail apart. The Lesser Antilles is a rich and diverse cruising ground with good anchoring.

An almost imperceptible breeze fluttered the tops of the waves as we made our departure from Pinney Beach. The current weather fax indicated a good, steady fifteen knot breeze with a long three foot ocean swell when we sailed out of the lee of Nevis. The sails hung limp as we motored the one mile from Pinney Beach to the southern tip of the island. Caution and close observation is required when sailing out of the lee of an island and entering ocean conditions. The hazards include sudden unexplained gusts accompanied by very turbulent sea conditions. I looked south as we rounded Nevis. Picking up the binoculars from the cockpit table I got my first look at true sea conditions.

"We aren't towing the dinghy this morning" I said joking to Wendy, passing her the glasses.

"I thought that the waves were going to be three feet?" Wendy asked.

"They will be three feet. We just have to get past the five foot bumpy ones. At least the wind and the swell are in our direction" I said.

While we were still in relatively mild conditions I handed Wendy the wheel and pulled in the dinghy, securing it tightly to the davits. In only a few hundred feet the ocean began to boil. I had a moment to yell "Hold on" before we were hit by the concentrated force of a strong trade wind being steered around the side of a cloud-topped volcano. Quest heeled down hard into the blue Caribbean. She was thrown violently onto her starboard rail.

"Shortening sail" I yelled over the shriek of the wind. Directly in front of Quest the sea was streaked with white foam. "Grab the hardtop and hold on as tight as you can" I said to Wendy as I took the wheel. Her knuckles turned white as she forcefully grasped the hardtop. "Look ahead. If we can make the next quarter of a mile, we're going to be OK."

"This is definitely not OK" Wendy yelled.

The ride was getting wet and wild. Water blasted straight up into the air every time Quest's bow was buried in a wave top. As the wind increased, the gunnels were buried in green water. With no time to think I reached through the spokes in the wheel and engaged the autopilot on the instrument cluster. Racing forward in the cockpit, I released the port mainsheet clutch. The boom slammed to starboard restrained only by the starboard mainsheet line. The mainsail spilled air and Quest came out of her near broach. My palms sweat as I clicked off the autopilot and took the wheel.

Glancing at Wendy, I said "That's a little better. Throw me that rag in the winch locker. This wheel's getting slippery. That was really no big deal" I said.

"Oh, that was no big deal? Well, Long John Silver, take a look below" Wendy said.

"Hold the wheel" I said.

I walked to the companionway ladder and stared into the cabin. The one hundred pound saloon table was lying on its side with the contents spilled over the cabin sole. "Oh no." I had been doing maintenance in the bilge the previous day and the screws that secure the table to the floor had been temporarily removed. When the job was finished I had not replaced the screws.

Turning around I looked at Wendy. "Hey, you forgot to tell me to screw down the table" I said.

"Right, you forgot to screw the table down. Good job" Wendy said flippantly.

"So where did you put the screws?" I asked Wendy.

"You put them in the nav table" she said opening the drawer in the side. "See?"

After spending the next twenty minutes wrestling the table back into position, screwing it down, restacking contents, and finally repairing a couple of scratches and dings with a few dobs of varnish I returned to the cockpit. Our brief encounter with nasty conditions was miles behind us. Winds were now holding steady at a very pleasant fifteen knots and the sea state was much improved. I re-trimmed the main and Quest bolted forward at a blistering 6.1 mph.

By noon we were eighteen miles from Nevis and only a mile away from the Kingdom of Redonda. Redonda's appearance is both unique and startling when viewed for the first time. It appears to be a gigantic sheer sided slab of volcanic rock that juts straight out of the sea to a vertigo inducing height of approximately 1000 feet.

The island is uninhabitable. It is a magnificent sight when sailing past. The absolutely vertical sides of the island give way to a top which slants precariously at about thirty degrees to the west. As we approached the island, the noon day sun glinted off the thick mat of green vegetation growing on the top. It gave the impression of a very odd looking giant's putting green.

Redonda is a stunning geological oddity and one of the largest piles of bird guano in the Western Hemisphere. It also holds a very small but special place in today's geopolitics. Claims on its sovereignty are shrouded in myth and fantasy. The island of Redonda is a micronation. Its official title is 'The Kingdom of Redonda'. A micronation is 'an independent nation or state which is not officially recognized by world governments'. The world's quota of micronations is very tiny, yet the stories behind these quasi sovereign nations are always bizarre. The history behind the Kingdom of Redonda is one of the most bizarre.

Currently the ownership of the Kingdom of Redonda is shared by a diverse group of one hundred people. The majority of the claimants to the island are the direct descendants of writer M.P. Shiell and his editor John Gawsworth. The other small group of claimants are people who believe that they are the reincarnation of Shiell or Gawsworth. The story of Redonda begins in the 1800's when M.D. Shiell, a Methodist lay preacher from Montserrat claimed the island for his son M.P. Shiell. Around 1850, M.D. Shiell (Senior) petitioned Queen Victoria for the title 'King of Redonda'. It is believed that the British Colonial Office under the authority of the

Queen granted Shiell the title if he and his successors pledged in perpetuity not to revolt against the colonial power of Great Britain. This in turn bestowed the title of Prince of Redonda onto Shiell's newborn son Matthew Phipps (M.P.) Shiell. M.P. Shiell grew up and became a well read writer of supernatural and scientific romance novels and short stories. The writer M.P. Shiell became the King of Redonda after the death of his father. On the death of the son the title of King of Redonda was bequeathed to Shiell's literary editor John Gawsworth. The ancestors of both Shiell and Gawsworth consider themselves the rightful monarchs of Redonda.

The Kingdom of Redonda has a navy. The Monarchy holds a royal court. The island has an anthem and even an official stamp. The 100 peers of the Kingdom of Redonda sincerely believe their claim is genuine. It is highly doubtful if anyone else outside their circle takes them seriously. The biggest doubters would certainly be the legislature of Antigua and Barbuda who genuinely believe that the island belongs to them. As Quest gently glided past Redonda on a choppy sea, we raised our glasses in salute to the island's royal family, wherever it might be. "Long live the King."

Today's anchorage was twelve miles ahead on the island of Montserrat. Little Bay on the northwest corner of Montserrat would be a snug place to ride out the tropical wave. There is little similarity between the islands of Redonda and Montserrat. Redonda has a very colorful claim to fame. Except for a few transient guano harvesters in the late 1800's, it has never been inhabited. It is just a very nice rock. Montserrat, on the other hand, has been continuously occupied for the last four thousand years. Archaeological discoveries suggest that the Arawak of South America were first to settle the island. Much later the Saladoid from the lowlands of the Orinoco River in Venezuela moved north to occupy many of the islands from Trinidad to Puerto Rico, including Montserrat. Christopher Columbus passed Montserrat during his second voyage to the Caribbean in 1493. He made no attempt to land or claim the island for King and country.

The task of possession and colonization of the island was left to the British in 1632. The British made great strides in agriculture during their occupation. Sugar cane production flourished with the help of a teeming population of slaves. Then cheap sugar imports from Brazil destroyed the British plantation owners' dreams of wealth. Montserrat remains a British crown colony to the present.

In more recent years, George Martin, the producer of the rock band 'The Beatles' built AIR Studios on Montserrat in 1979 to offer the rock music industry a unique place to produce and record music. For more than ten years AIR Studios hosted recording sessions for the who's who of rock and roll. Dire Straits, The Police, Paul McCartney, Elton John, Duran Duran, Michael Jackson, Stevie Wonder, Ultravox, The Rolling Stones, Lou Reed, Black Sabbath and Eric Clapton are just a few of the notables who produced albums on the island. Then on the 17th of September 1989, Hurricane Hugo struck with such force that ninety percent of the structures on the island were destroyed. AIR Studios closed and the tourist economy was wiped out.

Six years later the main volcano on Montserrat began to erupt. The island's capital, Plymouth, was buried in more than thirty-nine feet of mud and ash. The airport and docking facilities were destroyed. The southern half of the island was evacuated and considered uninhabitable. After several hundred years, the economy of Montserrat ground to a screeching halt within months. Today, virtually every single thing for sale on the island is imported. The island's tiny budget is provided by the British government.

Montserrat may not be the economic powerhouse that it once was but it still looked beautiful as we made our approach into Little Bay. Ever since the volcanic catastrophe buried the capital city of Plymouth, the smaller port of Little Bay has served as the commercial center of Montserrat. We slipped in quietly with a gentle land breeze. Fishing pirogues occupied the larger northerly side of Little Bay. There were only two sailboats in a small area set aside for visiting yachts. The anchor held strong. We were about two hundred feet from the beach over a gravel bottom.

By the time the sails and sea gear were neatly stowed it was slightly past four o'clock.

"Wendy? Does the guide mention how late Customs is open?"

She thumbed through the introduction to Montserrat. "No, it doesn't mention anything about Customs" she said.

"I'll radio the cruisers and see if anyone's home" I said. "Anybody in Little Bay, come in." The VHF radio was silent. I tried it again. "Does anybody know how long

Customs and Immigration is open today?"

I received a lightning fast response. "This is the
Montserrat Port Authority."

I looked at Wendy. "Port Authority?"

It is almost impossible to imagine a foreign official
contacting a sailboat. They consider it the responsibility of
the captain to arrive in person to Customs/Immigration
within a reasonable time. I was surprised by the message.

"Port Authority, this is the sailing vessel Quest. Can
you tell me when Customs and Immigration close for the
day?"

"You have one hour to report. Please be prompt"
the voice of Montserrat Port Authority warned.

I looked towards the Customs building on shore. "I
don't know what kind of a reception we're in for. But I
think we better get going."

I threw on my clean going-to-town tank top,
jumped into the dinghy with Wendy and raced for the
Government pier. The ferry from Antigua had just arrived
and was deboarding about thirty passengers.

"I guess they weren't in that big of a rush" I said to
Wendy.

We let the ferry passengers file in front of us. We
formed a long serpentine line that crept forward slowly for
about a half hour. Then it was our turn.

"Next" the officer said in a gruff tone as he waved
us forward. I placed our passports on the desk. "How long
was your stay in Antigua?" he snapped.

"Never been to Antigua" I said politely.

"This is the line for the ferry. Go over to that

window" he said pointing to a sign that read Commercial Vessels.

I walked up to the officer at the window. He gave me a big grin.

"So you met Grouchy" he said loud enough for the whole room to hear. "I'll see if I can be a little more hospitable" he said taking our passports. "Everything is in order" he said stamping the passports. "You're checked in and out."

"We got a call earlier from the Port Authority" I said.

He raised his hand dismissively. "Forget about their nonsense" he said. "Port Authority got a new radio tower two days ago. They're driving everybody crazy playing with their new toy. Enjoy your stay in Montserrat" he said shaking my hand and walking us through the lobby. "You won't have any trouble finding a ride if you need one" he laughed.

Seven cabs crowded the small parking lot in front of Customs. All of the drivers seemed content to sit behind the wheel of their freshly washed vehicles and casually solicit the ferry passengers walking by except for one lone driver at the back of the lot who appeared to be asleep.

Eleven

Brimstone on the Beach

Cabbies all over the world are most skilled in assessing potential cash flow. We watched as each driver took turns hustling the ferry passengers then drove them up the hill.

"Do you want to go for a walk before it gets too late?" Wendy asked.

There was still one taxi driver half asleep in the back of the parking lot. "Ride?" the driver said casually as we passed his open window.

"No. I think we'll walk" I said.

"Hill pretty big. Better I take you in car" he persisted.

I smiled and walked past. When we were a short distance up the hill, the cabby raced past us, honked his horn and waved.

"He's in a big hurry" I muttered under my breath.

We continued our uphill stroll on a dusty road with no particular destination in mind. When we passed the third switchback, we saw the driver on the shoulder of the road. Jumping out of his car he walked up to us and offered his hand.

"I bring you right to the Plymouth Exclusion Zone. You never seen anything like it" he said.

"No thanks" I said.

"Only one hundred dollars US" he said as we walked away.

Turning around I said "You want one hundred dollars for a five mile trip. Forget it."

"One hundred dollars too much?" he said with a surprised look on his face.

"Too, too much" I said.

"I really like you two. I give you great ride for fifty bucks."

Smiling, I shook my head 'no' and kept walking.

"Wait, wait, twenty-five dollars" he said.

"OK. That's the magic number" I said. "You've got a deal" I said.

"I'm Jonathan."

"David and Wendy" I replied.

He walked us back to the small Nissan sedan and gallantly opened the back door for Wendy. "We have great trip" he said adjusting the mirror and looking me in the eyes. He zoomed off south. "Dis Carres Bay. Dis post office" he said pointing to a drab building as we drove down an incline towards the ocean.

"Were you born on Montserrat?" I asked

"Me born on Antigua. Came 1978 with family."

"Do you like living on Montserrat?" I asked.

"Very good place. All family live here" he said rotating a collection of small photos hanging on a string of beads from the rear view mirror.

111

"Where you live?" he asked.

"Little Bay" I said.

"You bring family with you?"

"Of course. She won't let me go anywhere without her" I said pointing at Wendy.

We continued up a long dusty grade into the hills. At times the thick tropical vegetation formed a complete canopy over the road. Driving in and out of dappled afternoon sunshine we passed hundreds of gaily painted small houses and cottages set back only a few feet from the highway. Descending back towards the coastline Jonathan pulled over to the side of the road.

"Dis Olveston. I live here. That Salem" he said pointing south. "Dat Frith. Dat where we go today."

I caught Wendy's eyes and pointed to Frith on the tourist map. "Frith?" I asked "That's a long way from the Exclusion Zone."

"Yes, quite far. We be safe" he said turning off the divided road onto a one lane track that climbed steeply into the hills. The vegetation gently scraped both sides of the car as he inched forward into thick jungle. "Almost there" he said.

About the last thing I wanted that day was to be driven into the middle of nowhere by a taxi driver that I had met twenty minutes before. "Where are we going?" I asked insistently.

"We almost there" he said.

I leaned over to Wendy and spoke very quietly. "He can't turn around here. When I say jump, get out and run."

"We here, we here" he said enthusiastically looking

at me nervously in the rear view mirror. The car pulled in front of a small dilapidated one story shed.

"Get ready" I said opening the door. The sticky tropical heat hit me like a wall as I stepped out.

"One minute. You stay here" he said running around the back of the building. He returned seconds later carrying a short home made wooden ladder. Propping it against the side of the shack, he said "Go up on roof. It safe."

"OK" I said feeling apprehensive. I climbed the ladder, then Wendy, then Jonathan.

"Come, you see Exclusion Zone now" he said motioning us to the very edge of the crumbling building. "Look over there" he pointed.

"I don't see anything" Wendy said leaning over the roof's edge.

"Over there." Jonathan gently turned Wendy's shoulders to the southeast. "Look" he said.

If I stood on my tip toes I could almost make out a small piece of gray, barren ground about a mile in the distance. "That's the Exclusion Zone?" I said.

"Dis it. Great view, eh?"

"You have to be kidding" I said.

He looked down and seemed genuinely hurt. "OK. Dis not good? I bring you to airport tomorrow. My sister has friend who knows brother of man who fuels helicopter. You take air tour of Plymouth tomorrow, very stunning. Only three hundred dollars."

"OK Jonathan, why don't we get back in the car and talk about it" I said smiling.

113

Wendy and I stood beside the shack. While Jonathan attempted to turn the cab around in the small clearing, we gave him plenty of assistance with hand signals. A few moments later we were on our way down the goat path, parting the tight vegetation all the way.

"I take you to nice restaurant?" Jonathan asked.

"Thanks anyway Jonathan. Why don't you bring us to Little Bay. I'm going to cook on the boat tonight" I said.

"Sure mon. We be in Little Bay real soon."

I couldn't get that tiny postage sized view of the Exclusion Zone out of my thoughts.

"Jonathan, what was it like when the volcano erupted?" I asked.

"It bad, real bad, but not too bad. Many months to bury Plymouth. Everybody in north island take people into homes. Many leave island."

"Where did they go?"

"England mostly. Some move to Montreal."

"But you stayed."

"Yes, my family very lucky."

"Will the people come back?"

"They don't come back. They make new lives in new homes. British very good to Montserrat. They take many in but they also build new city on Montserrat. Community called Lookout on windy side built for people who lose everything" he said.

When the car slowed to a stop at the government pier Wendy gave Jonathan twenty-five dollars.

"Thanks for the ride" I said shaking his hand through the car window.

The government pier shined brilliantly from the hundreds of security lights pointing in every direction. As I pushed off the dock, I was so light-blinded that Quest was only a memory in the darkness.

"I think we should leave tomorrow and go anchor off Plymouth" I said pulling alongside Quest.

"You want to anchor in the Exclusion Zone?"

"Yeah, why not" I said.

Wendy shrugged.

I slept very uneasily that night. I kept waking and thinking about a city covered in ash a few miles south. Dawn couldn't come soon enough. Wendy finally got up. I was sitting in the cockpit with a cup of tea.

"You're in a big hurry" she said.

"There's some couscous with butter on the stove."

We filled up on warm cereal and discussed the day's plan.

"Plymouth is only about eight miles and there's absolutely no wind yet. I don't see the point of putting up the sails. Let's motor south along the coast. That way we can run the water maker for a couple of hours. If you get the dishes, I'll warm up the engine and get things ready on deck" I said.

Reaching over the steering wheel I turned the key in the ignition. A bang sounded from the lazarette. The engine was dead. 'That's odd' I thought lifting the seat and climbing down into the lazarette. I removed the high amperage fuse cover that runs from the starter batteries to the engine.

"Burnt" I said looking up at Wendy. "Get me

115

another fuse and the volt meter."

Where could the short be? Why was there a short? There couldn't be a short. We had used the engine less than twenty hours ago. I went through every single inch of wiring between the batteries and the engine. Then I did it a second time. Everything looked perfect.

"Hand me that new fuse. Maybe the old one went bad."

The fuse went bad? Fifty amp fuses don't go bad. There had to be a dead short somewhere. But a dead short in a #3 cable? It would have left scorch marks someplace. The replacement fuse was installed. I stepped back up into the cockpit and turned the ignition key. Bang. A metallic smell rose from the fuse box.

"How many more fuses do we have?"

"One" Wendy said holding out her hand.

I probed and prodded every inch of the jacketed cable from every angle with the Ohm meter.

"We've got a big problem here" I said laying down in the cockpit. "If we blow that last fuse, that's it for the engine."

"We could sail to Antigua and get a fuse" Wendy said.

"We could sail or take the ferry to Antigua, but that isn't the point. We could bring back a bag of fuses and it won't make any difference. I need to find the short. This is absolutely ridiculous. It's five feet of cable. Anybody can find a short in five feet of cable."

Frustrated, confused, and sweating, I jumped back into the lazarette. I began at the battery and ran my fingers around the wire in the direction of the engine starter. It took me almost an hour to feel every inch of the cable until it turned down towards the starter terminal. I needed to continue the job from the access hatch in the saloon.

"How's it going?" Wendy asked when I had one hand under the engine.

"This is unbelievable. There's no short. I'm sure of it" I said.

"What's a short again?"

"Forget it" I said.

There was only one foot of wire to check. I snaked my hand along the wire. I was hoping all the while that some insulation had frayed and the cable was shorting somewhere. As my hand groped closer to the starter, a solution to the problem was becoming more elusive. If I couldn't find a short in that cable, nobody would. 'Please. Let there be a short' I whispered under my breath.

I reached the starter terminal. "What's this?" I said.

Wendy was an inch behind me and breathing on the back of my neck. "What's what?" she said.

"The lug nut of the starter is loose" I said.

"Could that cause a short?" Wendy asked.

"No, a loose nut doesn't cause a short. It causes an open."

"What's an open?"

"It's the opposite of a short." I stood up and stretched my back. "It won't cause a short. But in a very high amperage circuit a loose nut will cause arcing which could blow a fuse."

117

I learned my lesson. Keep the lug nut on your starter tight.

Pulling out the ratchet set I snapped on a socket. "This ought to do it" I said cranking the nut for all I was worth.

Wendy handed me the last fuse and I screwed it into the fuse holder.

"Turn the key" I said from the lazarette.

"Me?" Wendy squeaked.

"Wendy, turn the key."

She tentatively sat behind the wheel. Her hand reached out for the key. "Maybe you should turn it."

"Just turn the key" I shouted.

She reached forward and gave it a twist. The engine roared to life.

Always have patience when working on anything on a cruising boat. What would take five minutes in your garage could take three hours on a boat. Space is normally so tight that you may not even be able to see what you are trying to repair. Be prepared to work exclusively by touch and feel. Some times an engine will have a dedicated space which makes repairs much easier. Most boats do not. Impellers, hoses, and in my case the nut on the starter are in dark inaccessible places where there is only room to squeeze in one hand. It is essential to be able to create a visual image of any object simply by feeling it. Very often that is all you will have. Just hope that the boat isn't sinking at the same time.

It was noon in June. Little Bay was getting extremely hot and stuffy.

"Let's get out of here" I said walking back from the bow after raising the anchor.

Wendy swung the bow. We began motoring the short trip south. The eastern coast of Montserrat is a dramatic combination of high cliffs that rise steeply into the hills of the Soufriere volcano. Small colorful houses liberally sprinkle the hill sides. At times they seem to be precariously perched along the cliff's edge. With no sails aloft we were able to pull in very close to shore and enjoy a unique view of a beautiful island framed by a turquoise sea. Close to Old Town, we got the first clue that we were entering the Exclusion Zone.

"Hey! Is that you?" I said to Wendy.

"No that is not me" Wendy said indignantly.

The sulfur smell was faint but definitely noticeable. "It must be the couscous" I said.

"That's no couscous" Wendy said. "Listen to this." She read from one of the Montserrat tourist brochures that we had picked up at the ferry terminal. "The Exclusion Zone was established in 1997. It includes two sea areas which are adjacent to the land areas. The dangers of volcanic eruption are real. The zone is for the protection of human life. The dangers include blown ash, volcanic explosion, pyroclastic flow and poisoning gasses. Now, that sounds like a real resort spot. Let's make sure we don't miss the poison gasses" she said looking up.

"I'll make sure we pass the gas" I said.

We motored up close for a good look at Fox Beach, then swung out to sea at Bransby Point. A gentle confused wave slapped at the bow. Rounding Bransby Point, we got our first look at Plymouth. Nothing could have prepared us for what we were about to see. The landscape was gray on gray.

"Take a look" I said handing Wendy the binoculars.

The three thousand foot high volcano was belching out a plume of white gas. Destruction extended from the craggy top of the volcano and fanned out on both sides to form a mile wide delta of mud and ash at the shoreline. The scene was frightening. I motored in closer.

"Let's anchor about two hundred feet off that dock" I said pointing to a structure in the mud.

It was a place like no other. A smell of sulfur wafted over the ruins. Quest's white decks soon began to collect a very fine powdery ash. The place was unworldly. Two hundred feet in front of us an entire city lay covered in gray ash. Apartment buildings, office buildings, houses and streets were all buried and completely lost. We stood dumbstruck on the bow and took in the spectacle. Within this great silence there was not a single sign of life, not a tree, not a blade of grass, not even a soaring bird. Evidence of the transient nature of man was everywhere. Grief flooded over both of us. Luckily the loss of human life in Plymouth was minimized. Yet the death of a city was right before our eyes.

The wind began to back to the east. The jets of steam and ash from the volcano began to drift in our direction.

"We're out of here" I said stepping on the windlass switch. "Put her in gear. We'll anchor at Fox Beach. It looked beautiful. That will keep us safe from the stink."

Brimstone on the Beach

Wendy turned Quest's nose around and made a hasty retreat. Fox Beach gave us perfect holding for the evening in soft sand.

Twelve

Leave the stink behind

$\mathbf{F}$ox Beach, Montserrat is very quiet and secluded. It is on the northern edge of the Montserrat Exclusion Zone. We had every expectation that our solitude would not be interrupted. As the sun began its quick descent, we threw our clothes into a heap on the cockpit floor and jumped into the warm crystal blue water. Crossing my ankles over the anchor chain, I looked up to catch a glimpse of the green hills that rose gently from the sandy beach. A few dozen very spacious mansions were tastefully set back from the road that crisscrossed the hill.

"I'm kinda surprised anyone would want to live this close to an active volcano" I said to Wendy.

Wendy turned towards the beach. She squinted and looked up the hill. "You're right. I wouldn't want to live this close to Plymouth. Isn't that area a part of the Exclusion Zone?" she asked.

"I'll take a look" I said climbing up the stern ladder into the cockpit. The chart of the Plymouth area was folded on the table. "I'm not sure if we're in the Exclusion Zone or not. We're right on the edge. I think we might be in the 'Daytime Entry Zone' whatever that is" I said.

Leave the stink behind

Picking up the binoculars I scanned the houses a quarter mile up the hill. "They're all abandoned" I said.

"Abandoned? They don't look abandoned" Wendy said climbing up the ladder into the cockpit.

"Well, take a look" I said handing her the binoculars.

"Yeah, it's a ghost town" she said.

We could make out thirty-five large residences terraced in a well planned enclave. Their pastel colored stucco exteriors and red tiled roofs still looked attractive in the rich gold-orange light of the setting sun. Blooming bougainvillea and bright red oleander espaliered along walls which separated the villas. Profusions of colorful tropical plantings grew in abundance along the roadsides. From all appearances it was a once beautifully planned Caribbean development gone to seed.

"Look at that real big house on the top of the hill on the right. It's been completely ransacked" I said passing Wendy the binoculars.

All of the windows had been smashed. Glass lay everywhere glittering like heaps of diamonds in the weeds. Overgrown vegetation grew in flourishes of green from the gutters. The red brick driveway that dramatically circled the front yard was a tangle of vines and thickets. Further down the hill, odds and ends of broken furniture lay scattered against a wall. The pool was filled to the top with a grayish-green soupy slurry. Gray volcanic ash was piled up like dirty snow in the doorway.

"There is probably more than a billion dollars worth of real estate on that hill" I said.

"Was" Wendy replied.

Only an hour ago we had gotten our first sight of the havoc that a volcano can bring. The desolation in Plymouth, a city covered in feet of gray ash and mud, was beyond comprehension. In comparison, the scene up the hill was quite different. It didn't fill me with the same dread as the Plymouth disaster. The inhabitants of the settlement had simply walked away, leaving their houses and possessions. With no power to stop them, looters had taken over. Then the relentless destructive effects of the tropical climate rapidly accelerated the decay.

"Do you want to buy some prime Caribbean real estate real cheap? Here's your chance. I see a very nice fixer upper over there" I said.

The sun slipped into the sea. Darkness engulfed us as we drank a cold beer in the cockpit and watched a smokey brown full moon rise lazily through the toxic plume of the Soufriere volcano. The bright moon soon dominated the evening sky. It arched towards its zenith, leaving a shimmering silvery trail as it reflected off the wave tops in the anchorage.

The reflective white sand on Fox Beach sparkled in the moon light. The gentle waves that broke on the shore were a glowing line of white foam against a black background. The entire settlement seemed to disappear into the dark hills. As the moon rose higher and higher, long shadows stretched out from the corners of the houses. Flecks of light reflected from the shards of glass lying beneath the broken windows. The sense of abandonment was complete. Then the spell of the eerie scene was suddenly broken by a pinprick of intense light coming from over the hill.

"Look David. I think there's a car stopped on the top of the hill" Wendy said as she handed me the binoculars.

"I think its an old Nissan truck" I said.

The headlights from the vehicle sent a momentary bright flash right into the cockpit. The driver made a slow descent of the hill.

"Night watchman?" Wendy speculated.

"I kinda doubt it. Who would pay someone to guard this mess?" I said. We lost sight of the truck as it weaved through the overgrowth. "There it is" I said.

"Yeah, it's right beside the house with the flat roof" Wendy said. "I see it."

The driver pulled around to the missing front door of the house and turned his lights off.

"Those dudes aren't the police" I said. "Look."

Two men in ragged shorts and tank tops got out of the truck, looked around suspiciously and entered the house. They reappeared in the entrance carrying a long dining room table with one leg missing.

"The picking must be getting pretty lean" I said.

"Should we call the police on the VHF radio?" Wendy whispered.

The two men tied the table down and sped off towards the beach.

"Yeah, I'll call the police."

I keyed the VHF microphone. Loud feedback squealed from the VHF cockpit speakers. I turned the volume control down and tried again.

The driver pulled the truck to the edge of the water and trained his headlights on Quest's bow. Both men jumped out and stood on the shoreline.

"Who dat out dere?" shouted the driver.

"What you want here?" said the other man.

"Now look what you got us into" Wendy whispered.

I slowly reached into the lazarette and pulled out the high intensity spot light and the megaphone. "When I give you the word, point the spot right in their eyes. Now" I said.

Wendy clicked on the spot and shined the light in the driver's eyes.

"Who dere?" the driver yelled angrily covering his eyes.

I squeezed the megaphone trigger. "Dis Montserrat marine patrol. Stop where you are."

My amplified voice echoed off the low sand bluffs on each side of the beach and sounded like the entire police force of Montserrat was about to make a sting. The two men scrambled towards the truck leaving sand flying from their shoes as they jumped into the cab. The truck's tires spun in the soft sand. The passenger jumped back out and pushed the truck from the ruts. Wendy kept the spot light trained on the vehicle until they had crested the hill.

"That was hilarious!" Wendy said.

"More fun than calling the police?" I asked.

"Way more fun" she laughed.

"The bigger problem is if the police showed up

they might have packed us off with the thieves."

"What?" Wendy said.

"We're in the Exclusion Zone, remember."

"Whoops, you're right" she said. "Do you think they'll be back?"

"They'll definitely be back. Just not tonight. Tonight they're going to a 'bring your own table' party."

It wasn't the apprehension of the free lance looters that kept me on the alert throughout the night. It was the constant smell of mild sulfurous fumes. Around two in the morning, the air atop the high mountain began to cool, right on schedule. Like most Caribbean islands with high peaks, the cool denser air begins a slide down the hills towards shore in the wee hours. This natural air-conditioning is always welcome unless one is downwind from an active volcano.

I woke up very early with clenched fists. I threw my legs over the side of the bunk. My head pounded as I fought off mild nausea. I shook Wendy. She rolled over and looked at me.

"You know you could have brought that outside" she said.

"It's worse out there."

"Wow, what did you put in that burrito?" she said rubbing her temples.

I tapped her on the leg. "I'm going to try to start the engine."

"Try, what's with the try, you still worried about the engine?"

"Worried, not me" I said clicking on the cabin light.

127

Stumbling up the companionway, I sat behind the wheel and tentatively twisted the ignition key. Varoom. I felt a brief moment of pride mixed with satisfaction.

"I knew I fixed it" I said to Wendy as she stepped into the cockpit.

"The diesel fumes smell like perfume compared to the volcano" she laughed.

"I'm pulling up the anchor. The sooner we get out of here the sooner we leave the stink behind. Keep us off the beach" I said.

Halfway to the bow I felt rough grit on the bottoms of my feet. I sat down on the cabin top and shined the light on my bare soles.

"Wendy" I shouted back to the cockpit. "Don't walk on the decks."

"Why not? What's going on?" she asked.

"They're covered in ash. There's also been a heavy dew. It's a real mess. Just stay off the decks or you'll grind it in. I'll wash the deck down when we're under way."

The hundred feet of anchor chain was hauled in and the anchor pinned.

"OK" I shouted.

Wendy kept Quest's bow into the light fluttering breeze while I raised the main.

"Oh no, turn on the spreader lights" I said stepping back and looking at the main.

We both let out involuntary groans as we looked up. There was a distinct crisscrossed pattern of black lines all over the starboard side of the white sail.

"The ash" Wendy said.

128

Leave the stink behind

"I don't think it's as bad as it looks. It will probably shake off after it dries" I said hopefully.

We motored a perpendicular course straight out from the beach until we felt the air begin to stir. About two miles from Montserrat we caught the trade wind. We were about to have a pleasant forty mile beam reach to the port of Deshaies on the north shore of Guadeloupe. The sun finally rose over the volcano of Montserrat just as the shoreline of the island was beginning to disappear from view. The odorous fumes of sulfur were dissipated by the strong southeast trade winds. We were out of the stink and on our way to France.

The islands of Guadeloupe and Martinique are not autonomous territories or independent nations like most of the other Caribbean islands. They have a much different political distinction. They are French soil, just as much as any part of the French mainland is France. Because Guadeloupe and Martinique are considered to be in France they follow all applicable French marine law. In regard to boat ownership and documentation, French marine law hasn't changed much since the reign of the Louis's. It is very strict and very lopsided in favor of France.

In the United States, the US Coast Guard issues a Certificate of Documentation to qualifying marine vessels. This document provides conclusive evidence of nationality and ownership which is universally recognized by world governments. To document a vessel in America, the owner must be an American or an American corporation. Wendy and I jointly owned Quest. Wendy is American. I am Canadian. Therefore Quest was ineligible for U.S. federal documentation. Quest only had a Florida state registration. State boat registration is similar to car registration. The vast majority of all the world's governments accept state documentation as proof of ownership.

France is one of the only exceptions. All boats entering French waters MUST possess international documentation issued by a country recognized by France. In theory only, French authorities require that all boats be documented, the document must be the original and it has to be current. If a captain can not produce proper documentation, the boat is immediately seized and becomes a 'prize' of the French Republic. There is no trial, no arbitration, no discussion. The French are very insistent and forceful on this point of law. If your boat is seized, the authorities will only allow you to take away your personal belongings. On becoming aware of this peculiarity of French law, I was in complete disbelief. I made inquiries with the US Coast Guard.

"Yes, have no doubt, the French can impound any boat without federal documentation. The French navy can even seize a boat on the open seas if the captain can not prove ownership. Ownership to French authorities can only be proven by documentation they recognize as legitimate."

So why would anybody in their right mind even consider sailing into Deshaies without proper papers? Deshaies is a very beautiful port on a particularly beautiful island. It is a small town with a quaint feel which deserves a visit. But, was it worth the risk of confiscation? It came as quite a surprise to find that the answer to that question was 'absolutely yes'. During our cruise south from Florida we ran into scores of captains who frequent French islands. It turns out that we would not be the first boat that sailed to Guadeloupe without federal documentation. Perhaps the most thorough and informative description of Deshaies' check-in procedures came from a delivery captain that we met in Luperon in the Dominican Republic. Over a cold beer and a discussion about Martinique and Guadeloupe, I told the captain that we would be skipping the French islands.

"Don't do that" he said. "They're fantastic." He spoke in detail about the size of the anchorages and where to find the best holding.

When he began to describe the restaurants and the night life I politely interrupted him. "If we go to Deshaies the French will confiscate our boat."

He leaned in close over the table. "So what are you smuggling? It must be pretty good."

"No, we aren't smuggling anything" I said with surprise.

"OK, so what's the problem?"

"Our boat only has state documentation."

"Big deal, so what's the problem?" he asked again.

"Boats must have federal documentation in French waters" I said.

"Absolutely" he said smiling. "Look I've been to Deshaies more than a dozen times. I was in Deshaies for a week at Christmas. Listen, what the French say and what the French do are two completely different things."

"That's easy for you to say. I bet all the boats that you captain have federal documentation" I said.

"That's true" he said. "I sail other people's boats for a living. I'm telling you, you won't have a problem in Deshaies."

"How can you be so sure?"

"I told you I've been to Deshaies a dozen times" he said. "Not only have I never checked in at Deshaies, I've never met anybody that has checked in. I met one captain that spent two days looking for the Customs dude. He finally caught up with the guy in a restaurant. He told him to get lost. Believe whatever you want. Nobody is going to take your boat in Deshaies, just as long as you don't try to check in."

Thirteen

A Dodge in Deshaies

There are many obvious differences between the waves that form in the North Atlantic and those formed in the Caribbean. The wind and storm generated waves in the North Atlantic often possess long swells with deep wide troughs. Big waves in the big Atlantic travel unimpeded for thousands of miles. A typical twenty foot wave in the Atlantic may have an enormous peak to peak spread of over a hundred feet. Sailing up and down the sides of twenty foot waves that are spaced out every hundred feet is an absolutely spectacular experience. The sheer size of the waves can overwhelm your imagination and test your resolve. Fortunately the big waves are rarely lethal unless your heart gives out from the adrenaline.

After these monster waves roll across the Atlantic their energy is eventually absorbed by an opposing shore. Most of the wave energy that crosses the Atlantic between the Bahamas and South America will strike a Caribbean island. A small percentage of the overall wave energy squeezes between the archipelago of islands. Nonetheless, a huge amount of energy still passes between the islands. The magnitude and shape of the recombined wave is altered considerably.

The waves in the Caribbean have notably smaller and more variable peaks and troughs. Spacing and magnitude are reduced. Dissonance is introduced. Caribbean waves are manifestly more lumpy and bumpy than their North Atlantic counterparts. When the waves meet on the western side of the islands they recombine to create thousands of different waves. All these new waves will travel in different trajectories. This makes for a confused sea noted by triangular topped waves that seem to move in multiple random directions. This confused sea makes for a rough, wet, unpredictable and teeth-jarring ride that can be rather uncomfortable.

Within an hour of leaving Montserrat, the wind settled into a constant twenty knot breeze directly on the beam. We had all the wind we needed to cover the forty mile journey in record time. It was the particularly confused sea that slowed us down. Although our course was straight from start to finish, our overall speed was held in check by Quest's bow plunging deeply into the huge green triangular waves that came at us from every side. It was a white knuckle, bone shaker of a forty mile ride. Nine hours later we unceremoniously sailed into the calm lee of the island of Guadeloupe just a few miles from Deshaies. It was another normal day in our Caribbean paradise.

The GPS soon sounded the two mile warning. A huge threatening black cloud hung over the hills south of Deshaies.

"They're getting a bad storm" Wendy said.

A Dodge in Deshaies

"Maybe we'll just hang back a bit. It should pass pretty soon" I said.

There was something very ominous and threatening about the storm cloud. The intensely black and gray clouds swirled and twisted and almost appeared to be alive inside. In less than thirty seconds the black squall line had spread out to the horizon and was pushing straight for us at an unbelievable speed. I stared for a moment in disbelief as the first drops of rain lashed at my upper body.

"Uncleat the jib line and let it luff, right now" I yelled.

Leaping to the cabin top I wrapped one arm around the mast, slid to my knees and uncleated the main halyard. The heavy full battened cruising sail dropped smoothly into the lazy jacks. The rapidly increasing wind slowed Quest and pushed her off course.

"Turn on the engine, full throttle. Keep her into the wind" I yelled.

Looking through the windscreen I caught Wendy's eyes. She gave me a thumbs up. Holding on to the mast with one arm I reached up and removed my hat and stuffed it under my waistband. Then my world became engulfed in a dark fury of wind, water and grayness.

"Keep her straight. Keep her straight" I yelled over the shrieking wind.

A gust of spray and wind pushed me against the mast. Then the storm gave a second lash and it was over that quickly. Mercifully the wind and rain stopped as if a switch had been thrown. I looked over my shoulder to see sunshine and blue sky over Guadeloupe and the storm

135

flying out to sea. I retrieved my dry ball cap from my shorts, placed it on my head and walked proudly back to the cockpit. Wendy had a big grin on her face.

"What?" I asked dripping all over the cockpit.

"I did pretty good, eh?"

"Sure you did. You did real good" I said.

"You did pretty good yourself. Look how dry you kept your cap" Wendy said continuing to steer north up the coast of Guadeloupe.

"Where are we going today?" I said.

"Aren't we going to Deshaies?"

"If we're going to Deshaies, master mariner, then you better turn around. Try going south."

"Oops" she said stepping away from the wheel.

Taking the wheel I gave it a couple turns to starboard and spun Quest around. Reaching over I tapped the throttle, reducing the rpm to a low throb.

"Before we commit ourselves to Deshaies we'll stay back a mile outside the harbor entrance and check it out. If we get any weird vibe, then we can keep sailing."

In minutes we had coasted to a dead stop at the harbor entrance. The port in Deshaies is two miles wide at the entrance and about two miles long. On the chart it looks somewhat square. Most of the anchorage is deep with a number of pockets of good holding on each side. We bobbed in the surf and studied the harbor.

"What do you think?" Wendy asked.

"I don't know. It looks pretty wide open. It's going to be hard to find anywhere to hide. This is one of the rare times I hoped for a crowd." I looked at the chart. "I think we need to anchor there, behind the docks" I said pointing to the south of the harbor. "If we anchor there, maybe Customs won't see us."

Who was I kidding? If they wanted to see us, then they had already seen us, even from this far out.

"Let's keep our heads down and get going" I said.

Our first of eight anchor drops was a short distance from the municipal docks at the far south of the harbor. For twenty minutes I dropped and re-dropped the anchor in four different spots. I tried and tried but I just couldn't find holding.

"Let's try the other side of the anchorage" I said.

"Do you think anybody's noticed us yet?" Wendy laughed.

I grinned and swung Quest around to the northeast corner of the anchorage. After another half hour of ripping furrows in the bottom, I gave up.

"I don't think we've ever had so much trouble anchoring" I said.

It was getting late in the afternoon. What do we do? The only place in the anchorage that we hadn't tried was a spot directly in front of Deshaies' downtown district.

"This is great" I said when the anchor finally held.

We had spent the best part of two hours motoring all over the Deshaies anchorage. We couldn't have been more obvious. Then in case someone missed us, we anchored dead center in the harbor and a stone's throw away from Customs.

"The one thing in our favor is that if Customs has been watching us they're probably laughing by now."

"I thought Deshaies was supposed to be one of the busiest sailboat ports in the French Caribbean. Where are all the boats?" Wendy said. "Do you want me to put up the quarantine flag?"

"No way. A quarantine flag will really draw attention. Don't worry about it. More boats will show up later" I said.

I was trying to look busy and nonchalant while I polished the stainless and kept a watchful eye on the government dock.

"Ahoy Quest!" I turned around to see a dinghy coming alongside. "I'm Joe. This is my wife Patrice. That's our boat Amethyst over there. We're Americans."

"Nice to meet you" I said spraying my polishing cloth with a light coating of oil.

"We noticed you came in a while ago. Have you checked in yet?" Joe asked.

I looked at Wendy who was pretending to polish the bow pulpit stainless.

"Uh, no" I said.

"Well we're going into town. You want to join us?" he said.

"Not right now" I said holding up the oily rag. "We'll check in later, when we're finished here."

"Oh. We haven't checked in either" Patrice said. "We came in three days ago. We've gone to Customs every day. The first day we went twice and stayed for hours. Every time we went, there was the same sign on the door."

"That's right. Why would they put a sign on the door that says 'DEMAND'?" Joe asked.

A Dodge in Deshaies

"Demand?" I said.

"Yeah, I'm pretty sure it said demand. Didn't it Patty?" he said.

"Are you sure that it didn't say 'DEMAIN'?" I asked.

"Yes, yes, demain. That's it. We just figured they couldn't spell. You know these island people" Patrice said.

"You say the sign's been up for three days?" I asked.

Joe looked at Patrice. "Yeah, it was three days, I think."

"If the sign's been up for three days, I wouldn't bother going back" I said. "'Demain' means 'tomorrow' in French.

Joe and Patrice looked at each other and both laughed. "My high school French is a bit rusty" Joe admitted.

"Well, you two have a great time in town. Demain" I said waving my polishing rag. They both looked at me with a blank expression. "Tomorrow" I said.

"Right, if we stay in Guadeloupe long enough we're bound to pick up a lot of French" Patrice said smiling and pushing their dinghy off.

Joe raced towards the dinghy dock. Fifty feet away, he made a quick u-turn and returned to Quest's gunwale.

"I almost forgot" he said. "The reason we came over was to tell you that there's a big sailboat race from English Harbor to Fort-de-France. The first leg of the race is to Deshaies. We just heard about it on the radio. They should start arriving in about an hour. The restaurants will be mobbed in a couple of hours."

Quest in the Caribbean

"Are you sure that you don't want to come with us?" Patrice asked.

"Thanks anyway, this will give you a chance to practice your French" I said.

Joe and Patrice motored off.

"Did you hear what he said? I asked Wendy.

"What?"

"We've got a bigger problem than Customs. Joe just said there's about fifty French boats coming from Antigua. They're going to be here in less than an hour."

"Oh no. Should we pull up and leave?" she asked.

"It's too late for that. Just put out all the fenders."

The sight of one French flagged sailboat coming into a harbor is enough to trigger a flight response in most cruisers. Fifty French boats on their way from Antigua is a red alert. The French have sailing traditions that rival any nation in the world. The French navy is modern, highly motivated and capable of defending French assets around the world. The French merchant navy carries billions of tons of cargo with minimal loss. Professional French sailboat crews are formidable. The boat yards of France are renowned. With all this wealth of history and skill, why can't the French learn to anchor? Wendy and I cringed every time we saw a French flagged vessel drop the hook. Every liveaboard in the Caribbean has a colorful repertoire of favorite French boater stories. Our afternoon in Deshaies was to become another story for the 'vaults of the absurd'.

"Here we go" Wendy said. "The carnival has just arrived."

A Dodge in Deshaies

I looked towards the entrance where fifty boats jockeyed to be first into the mouth of the anchorage. It looked like sailboat bumper cars. A blurring mass of identical ten meter boats with pendants streaming darted in every direction. As they raced closer we could here the echoing cheers and jeers of the competitors.

"Where's the finish line?" Wendy asked.

"It's probably the entrance buoy."

"Then the race is over?"

"I would guess that the race has been over for ten minutes. Now they're racing to see who gets the first seat at the bar" I said laughing.

Two boats sprinted straight down the center of the anchorage. They slowed to a crawl in light air. Less than one hundred feet from Quest's stern, the upwind boat gained a small lead and the crew cheered. Neither boat would give up an inch of space. Both captains appeared oblivious that they were on a collision course with Quest.

"This is going to be too close" I said reaching over and turning on the engine.

The two approaching sailboats lightly touched hulls as they slowly crept towards Quest's starboard quarter.

A crew member at the bow of the upwind boat screamed for my attention. "Move, move, get out of the way!"

"This is absolutely outrageous" I said clicking the transmission into forward and gunning the engine.

Quest eased forward two feet. The first boat crossed our stern. The crew member at the bow threw the anchor over the side fifteen feet from our gunwales. Their sails luffed. Everyone on board shouted victory. I turned around just in time to see the competitor pass within a hair's breath of our starboard side. I heard their anchor plop in the water, then the unmistakable feel of their anchor getting hung up on Quest's anchor chain. I put the transmission in reverse and went to full throttle. Quest backed hard and fast. Our anchor chain went rigid. Running to the bow I saw that one of the flukes of their anchor had caught our chain.

"You snagged my anchor chain" I yelled.

The crew of the boat milled about their deck oblivious. I lowered the dinghy, jumped in and paddled frantically to the bow.

"Get to the bow Wendy" I yelled.

The two chains were just beginning to intertwine.

"Help me" I yelled to the deck of the racing boat.

One of the crew turned to me, shrugged and smiled. Everything was cool with him. I untied the dinghy's painter from the bow and threaded the end into the eye of their anchor. Then I threw Wendy the other end of the painter line. She wrapped it around the windlass drum and engaged the windlass deck switch. The painter line went taut and began pulling the stem of their anchor out of the water. A moment later I heard the windlass stop.

"David, David" Wendy shouted. I looked up. "We've got a problem. The line's all wrapped around the windlass. It won't move."

"Don't worry about it" I said heaving the racing boat's chain and anchor into the bottom of the dinghy. "I've got it" I said sitting back on the seat panting.

A Dodge in Deshaies

Red faced I started to row towards the bow of the racer. Some one had finally gotten the attention of the boat's captain. He ran to his bow.

"What are you doing with my anchor?" he yelled.

Taking a good hold of the anchor's stem and fluke, I raised it over my head and threw it over their starboard rail. A great glob of brown mud dropped off the anchor leaving a nasty streak oozing down to the scupper. Taking the rest of their anchor chain in two hands I threw it over the side of the dinghy. The entire crew was now standing at their bow glaring down at me.

"Thanks for the help" I said giving their boat a shove away from Quest.

" American! Who do you think you are?" came the angry reply from the French captain.

Fourteen

A Wicked Wind

Deshaies was soon overrun with French racing boats arriving from Antigua. Wendy and I sat on the cabin top and watched the anchoring spectacular.

"Just throw the anchor over the side and dinghy away" Wendy laughed.

Each new racing boat that entered the harbor motored directly for the rapidly increasing ring of boats that was beginning to encircle Quest. Boat after boat wedged in on every side of Quest. Anchors were casually tossed overboard like bags of garbage. Not one captain set the anchor. Not one captain even cared. They were French, young, full of adrenaline and ready for fun. The crews stayed on the boats only long enough to remove their wet gear. Then they raced for the rum in their rubber dinghies.

"There is one up side to being surrounded by fifty boats" I said.

"There's an up side to this?" Wendy said.

"Yeah. Customs left town."

"But how are we going to get out of here tomorrow? That boat in front of us is right over our anchor" Wendy said pointing toward the bowsprit.

"Don't worry about that boat. I'm worried about these four" I said pointing at both sides of Quest. "If the wind blows from the north, those two boats will be over our anchor. But if the wind swings around from the south, then those boats will be over the anchor. Whatever way the wind blows we'll be waking up at least one hungover Frenchman tomorrow morning."

The smoke of all the outboard engines created a blue cloud that trailed all the way to shore. Within twenty minutes, a ring of bobbing dinghies obscured the Deshaies dock. The hills towering over the anchorage began to cast long shadows on the beach. Darkness fell.

A night of celebrating was getting under way. Bright strings of Christmas lights festooned the restaurant interiors giving the entire waterfront a warm festive glow. The twinkling pinpoints of red, gold and blue lights reflected off the wave tops and sparkled off the boat hulls. On shore it was standing room only. The old well-worn restaurants, bars, and rum shops were overflowing with loud party goers. As the evening went on, the amplified beat from dozens of loudspeakers blended into a homogeneous drumming. Quest's hull vibrated from this acoustic mixture of overlapping Caribbean rhythms. The party on land lasted late into the next morning when the Christmas lights in the bars were turned off. Groups of twos and threes returned to their boats continuing to party on their foredecks.

Our fitful sleep was thankfully over when the welcome tropical morning sun finally peeked over the hills.

Quest in the Caribbean

I arose to find garbage strewn everywhere. Beer cans, wine bottles and plastic litter bobbed about the flotilla of anchored boats. Crew members that had been forgotten or abandoned the previous night slept in twos at the shoreline. Unmanned and untethered dinghies floated haphazardly about the anchorage with their painters dangling in the water.

"What a mess" I said reaching down with the boat hook and pulling a plastic bag off Quest's engine intake. "Now it's our turn to make some waves." I started the engine then walked to the bow to evaluate our escape options. "What do you think?" I said to Wendy.

"It could be worse."

"Maybe we should wait till they leave in a couple of hours" I joked.

"No way" Wendy said emphatically.

The wind had shifted ever so slightly in the night and Quest was pointing to the north. The new problem was that the anchor chain ran out from the bowsprit then disappeared directly underneath a racing boat's hull. A second and third boat were only a few feet from our port and starboard rails.

"I think we need to back up hard and put some tension on this anchor chain" I said pointing down. "When the anchor chain lifts up, it's going to hit the bottom of this boat in front of us. If I back up hard enough, the anchor chain will push the boat over there" I said pointing right.

I went back to the cockpit and gunned the engine in reverse. The chain went bar tight. We heard the distinctive underwater scraping sound of a chain riding up the side of a hull. The boat in front of us moved smartly to the right.

"It's working" Wendy said.

The anchor chain popped out of the water with a snap.

"That was the easy part. Now we're going to have to get out of this parking lot" I said.

I gave Quest a small forward thrust then put her in neutral. Running to the bow, I winched in the chain and pulled up the anchor. Our bowsprit was inches from the racer's topsides.

"Get a fender over there quick, before we bump that hull" I said.

I picked up the boat hook and ran over to where Wendy was fending off the boat. I gave it a hard shove and it drifted away from Quest. The boat hook snagged on the lifeline and then rebounded against the cabin top. A loud pinging sound echoed. That finally did it. A very hungover and angry captain poked his head out of the companionway.

"Would you mind helping me? Your boat was over our anchor chain" I said.

"No. Keep the noise down" he said dropping out of sight into the cabin.

I pulled the anchor into the rollers and pinned it. Jumping back into the cockpit I said to Wendy "Pierre wants you to keep the noise down."

With the anchor at the bowsprit, I let Quest drift while I came up with a plan.

"This is really tight. Look at those two boats blocking us off. We're going have to make a u-turn right here. Take those fenders and hold them there and there" I said pointing to the starboard stern quarter.

I shifted into forward, cut the wheel all the way to starboard and slowly closed the gap between the boat off our port stern.

"Here we go."

I brought up the rpm. Wendy dropped the fenders between the hulls. The fenders began to bulge. I went to full rpm. Quest's momentum pushed the boat to the left.

"It's working. OK fender girl, watch the paint job."

With a long engine thrust, Quest pushed the boat even further. I eased back on the throttle. After a shift to reverse and a shift to forward, we were turned around. Yet another naked captain came out of his companionway screaming.

"What is wrong with you Americans? Are you all insane?" he yelled.

"I'm not an American, I'm a vegetarian" I yelled.

Maneuvering Quest through the knot of anchored boats, we safely made it to the harbor mouth. We stared back into the inner harbor with disbelief.

"It sure looks like a lot more boats when you're out here" Wendy said.

"This has gotta be some kind of record. Only a boatyard should be allowed to wedge fifty boats into a twenty boat space. I'm glad that's over" I said getting up to raise the main.

"Hey, look" Wendy said pointing south along the coast. "Isn't that Amethyst up there?"

"I think you're right. Give them a call while I raise the main." I caught the last few words of their conversation while I was returning to the cockpit. "I thought they were going to stay a day or two" I said.

"Their plans changed big time last night."

"What happened?"

"They didn't have a good night. A boat came in late last night and banged into their bow. By the time they got out of the cabin, the boat was long gone."

"Any damage?"

"Just a little bit of chipped paint. Otherwise everything's fine."

"Where are they headed?"

"Patrice said they're going to try for Dominica. I told her we're going there today."

"Good, we'll see them tonight" I said.

When things settled down, Wendy and I sat back in the cockpit and enjoyed a cup of hot chocolate as the island's rugged coastline reeled by. The west coast of Guadeloupe is magnificently grand. The jagged coastline is a delight for the eyes. Thousands of inlets and tiny bays interspersed with small inviting strips of white sand beach stretch for mile upon mile. The foothills seem to pop straight out of the turquoise sea. Further inland they rise up to meet the very high mountainous volcanic terrain. No matter where your eyes wander over this incredible tropical diversity, they will be drawn back to Grande Soufrière, the five thousand foot volcano which dominates land and sea.

Guadeloupe was first settled by the Arawak Indians. The Arawaks were an indigenous people from South

America. Around 300 AD, they populated most of the islands in the Lesser Antilles. The peaceful Arawak thrived for well over a thousand years until the more hostile and warlike Carib Indians from South America came to Guadeloupe and wiped them out. Columbus landed on his second voyage and claimed the island in 1493. The Carib proved very resistant to European colonization. The Spanish conquistadors unsuccessfully warred on the Carib Indians for hundreds of years. With each new Spanish campaign, the conquistadors were repelled and pushed back to the sea.

The French later claimed Guadeloupe in the early 1600's. The French were much more successful in obliterating the Carib Indians. Over the span of the next two centuries the island became an important source of field crops and slavery. Plantations thrived under French management, making Guadeloupe the most prosperous island in the Lesser Antilles in the 19th century. After slavery was abolished in 1848, the plantation owners imported Indian and Chinese indentured laborers. Today's predominantly Black African, East Indian and Chinese population reflects the island's history of slavery and servitude.

The economy on the island never recovered from the abolition of slavery and slumping commodity prices in the late 1800's. Eventually the growers regained some of their economic footing by concentrating on sugar cane which was used for the production of rum. Today practically all manufactured products are imported from France. In turn, Guadeloupe exports all of its vast agricultural output back to France. The island produces pineapple, coffee, cocoa, plantain, squash, yams as well as an abundance of tree fruits and flowers. Rum production and export remains a major staple of the economy.

Guadeloupe has a distinctly different geography than any other Caribbean island. Although it may look like a big butterfly-shaped island on a map of the Caribbean, Guadeloupe actually consists of the two sizable islands of Basse-Terre and Grande-Terre. A very narrow channel of water called the Salt River runs between them and separates the two islands. Guadeloupe is the largest land mass in the Lesser Antilles. It is also the home of the active volcano Grande Soufrière which is the largest mountain peak in the Lesser Antilles. The extensive land mass of the island and the height of the volcano combine to exert an astonishing influence over the trade winds that blow across the islands.

"Hey, listen to this" Wendy said reading from the cruising guide. "Sailors on the west coast of Basse-Terre need to to be prepared for radical wind shifts at any moment."

"What do they mean by radical wind shift?"

"I know it sounds a little bit far fetched but apparently the wind can swing 180° in a matter of minutes."

"Maybe they're talking about a gust of trade wind when we sail around the bottom of the island."

"It talks about that too. The wind reversing is something different. I think they're saying that the trade winds get trapped between the islands. This sets up some sort of vortices. If the vortices are strong enough, they suck the wind back toward shore through the mountain passes."

I picked up the chart. "I wouldn't worry about the great sucking wind too much We're already past Bouillante" I said getting up to stretch.

Picking up the binoculars, I looked forward to survey conditions ahead. Amethyst was the only boat in view about a mile ahead. I keyed the VHF mic.

"Amethyst, this is Quest. How's the wind holding?" I said over the radio.

"The wind's holding pretty steady at fifteen knots from shore" Joe answered.

"Have you noticed any wind shifts or gusts?" I said winking at Wendy.

"No, not yet. We must have the same guide. We were just reading about the big reversing vortex. It sounded a bit flaky."

"Well, if you notice anything give us a call" I said.

"Will do. Over and out" Joe replied.

A few minutes later I put the binoculars to my eyes to observe Amethyst's sail trim.

"Wow, they're catching some very heavy surf."

A moment later Amethyst's mast swung to a starboard tack and she began to heel dangerously.

"They're out of control. The wind shift is for real."

The waves started getting ugly. Amethyst's bow rose, then slammed heavily into a foaming wave sending a fountain of water over the boat. We watched in horror as Amethyst's radical heel brought the mast closer and closer to the sea until finally the tip of the spreader clipped the top of another enormous wave.

"Hold on Joe, steer into it" I thought to myself.

For a moment Amethyst appeared to be righting herself. Then her spreader tip dipped back down into the wave carving a deep groove in the water.

"If they don't do something they're finished."

Then we heard a pop and a tear.

"Did you hear that?"

"Take a look" Wendy said.

Amethyst's jib had blown out and was whipping to leeward. She had righted herself but the damaged sail continued to rip in two. The luff was still connected to the head stay but the leach was waving in tatters over their cockpit.

I reached forward and let off the main sheet brake, then eased the jib line.

"Turn on the engine" I called.

The same wind hit us like a wall. The boom slammed to port and the jib sheet flew through the sheet block.

"Quest, come in Quest. We've got a problem" Joe said over the VHF.

I could hear Patrice screaming in the background.

"We're about five minutes behind you. Hold on" I said.

Within a hundred feet the freak wind dissipated and was blowing off shore again. I trimmed the sails and motored alongside Amethyst. Patrice sat in the cockpit with a shocked look on her face.

"Do you need some help?"

"Not really. We're just shook up" Joe said.

"Do you want me to take a look at your starboard spreader? It hit the water pretty hard."

"Please."

I picked up the binoculars and scanned their rig.

"The spreader looks fine. But drop your jib before it gets beat to shreds. Other than that you look pretty solid. I'm going to fall off now. The water's a bit rough. Call us if you need help" I said.

"Thanks, we'll be OK" he said.

We kept two hundred feet behind Amethyst until we reached Vieux Fort at the bottom tip of the island where the wind veered sharply to the southwest. I looked at the chart.

"With this wind we'll need more than a few tacks if we want to make it to Portsmouth by dark. Îles des Saintes is less than ten miles away. The Saints will give us a good angle for Portsmouth tomorrow."

I called Joe back on the radio. "We're going to Îles des Saintes. Want to come?"

"No. We're going on to Rodney Bay to get the sail repaired."

Wendy and I waved at Joe and Patrice as our boats took their separate courses.

"What are we going to do about French Customs in the Saints?" Wendy asked.

"It's the Saints. What could possibly go wrong?"

Fifteen

Saint Crusty

Îles des Saintes is a grouping of several idyllic tropical islands ten miles south of Guadeloupe. The howling wind that blew us around the bottom of Guadeloupe pushed against an opposing current that raised the waves into foaming breakers. An hour of rough sailing put us in the lee of Îlet à Cabrit, a small island just north of the larger island of Terre-de-Haut. Safely behind the calm of Îlet à Cabrit, we got our first good glimpse of the anchorages at Îles des Saintes. A small scattering of fishing pirogues bobbed gently in the cobalt blue water which lapped against the city breakwall. All was quiet. On shore, low red roofed buildings and cottages crowded the palm lined waterfront. Mansions and hovels dotted the parched slopes further up the hills. With a bit of imagination the well worn facades easily transported me back to the 18th century.

The arid climate of Îles des Saintes give the islands a much dryer appearance than Guadeloupe. The low volcanic terrain receives only a fraction of the rain that its larger neighbor receives. Agriculture never prospered on these small islands. While Basse-Terre and Grande-Terre became plantation powerhouses in the 18th and 19th centuries, Îles des Saintes remained a low-key settlement of Bretons and Normans. Only a small number of black slaves were brought onto the islands as domestic help. Eventually the Europeans and Blacks interbred on these isolated tiny islands to form very tight communities that speak a culturally unique French patois called Saintois.

We dropped the sails a mile west of the waterfront village. Even though the Îles des Saintes Customs officers were reputed to be even laxer than Guadeloupe, there still was no reason to test the resolve of the authorities.

"Let's anchor as far away from the city as we can" I said picking up the chart.

"Pain de Sucre looks good. Even better, it looks deserted" Wendy said pointing west.

We dropped the anchor in the delightfully calm cove which was fringed with red tinted sand. We found very good holding in a powdery sand bottom.

"This is more like it. What a difference from last night. It would be pretty funny if this turns out to be the second leg of the Antigua to Fort de France race" Wendy said.

"They won't be coming here. We're way too far from the bars. Hey, that gives me an idea. Maybe when it gets dark we should dinghy into town and buy a baguette."

"You'd risk going to jail just to buy a baguette? Are you crazy?" Wendy asked.

"OK, how about a couple of chocolate raspberry tarts with whipped cream" I said.

"OK, when do you want go?" she asked.

"Hold on. Dessert has to wait a while. I need to make supper first" I said.

Every sailor who has overcome their fears of venturing far from home carries a special dream that must be carefully nurtured. This dream can only stay alive and thrive if we make it succeed. A sailboat on a big sea is a tiny world in a hostile universe. Simple comforts can ease the hardships and keep us on a straight course for success. The creature comfort of a good meal sustains the sailor's spirit. Good food has the power to nurture the dream of finding paradise. Without good food, the lonely sea can seem an endless desert where there is no escape. Good food has the power to fill the sailor with the hope of a tolerable journey. The big problem on a small sailboat is that good food can quite often be hard to come by. The fresh and delectable food on any cruising boat can dwindle in a matter of weeks. If food be the fuel that keeps the dream alive, then improvisation in the galley is key to a successful cruise.

Staring out at the Islands of the Saints through the open galley porthole, I could almost taste the fresh bread only a short dinghy ride away.

"Do you remember those great croissants we used to buy on that corner in Montmartre?" I asked Wendy.

"Sure. I remember them very well. You're going to make croissants? That would be great."

"No croissants tonight. We don't have any butter" I said.

"You aren't still thinking about going ashore, are you?"

"Not really. We are pretty low on fresh supplies. But

I'm not quite desperate enough to get busted for buying butter." I opened the top of the refrigerator. "I think you can throw this over the side" I said handing Wendy a plastic bag with some soft, slimy vegetable matter inside.

"What's this?" she said holding it up with two fingers.

"Fermenting celery."

"Gross" she said.

"Throw it out unless you want me to make some soup."

Wendy quickly climbed to the cockpit, opened the bag and dropped the contents overboard. "The fish liked it" she said. "What else should go?"

I opened a quart container of cottage cheese and smelled it. "Where did we buy this?" I asked.

"Nevis."

"Well, it might be OK if we cook it enough. Put it in the strainer and drain off the cream. I'll use the curds separately" I said. "We've got three carrots, a handful of raisins and a small container of chopped black olives. Hey, here's some pickled jalapeño too. How much flour do we have?"

"Quarter bag of flour" Wendy replied.

I opened the cabinet by the stove and pulled out a packet of bread yeast. "We're getting there" I said placing a saucepan of water on the burner. "Peel these carrots and I'll parboil them. Now we need a bit of substance. Get out some of the dried potato slices that we never use."

"They're under the settee table. Just a minute" Wendy said handing me the peeled carrots.

I dropped the carrots into the boiling water with a handful of the dehydrated potatoes. While the water boiled I re-hydrated the yeast in a half cup of warm water and a teaspoon of sugar. About a cup of flour was added to a mixing bowl with the starter, some salt and the cream from the drained cottage cheese.

"The carrots look done. Drain them. Put the potatoes aside and then rough grate the carrots."

"OK" Wendy said.

After the dough was kneaded I placed it back in the bowl to rise. "We're just about ready to put it together."

"Put what together?"

"Carrot, raisin, cheese curds, potatoes, pickled jalapeño and a dough ball. Guess what it is."

"No idea. Give me another clue" she said.

"Oh, I'm missing the most important ingredients: a pinch of oregano, basil and some pepper flakes."

"Right, that explains everything" she said sarcastically. So what's it called?"

"The ills of saints?"

"That's awful. Work on the name" Wendy said.

"How about a potato carrot pie?" I said.

"Not bad" she mused. "But you can do better."

I rolled out the dough into two sheets and placed one sheet in the bottom of a greased frying pan and trimmed the edges. I tossed the grated carrots and herbs together to make up the first layer, followed by the potato slices, cheese curds and finally the raisins, black olives and jalapeños. The top layer of dough was placed over the vegetables. The edge was trimmed and crimped. Before placing the lid on the pan I gave the crust a light coating of olive oil and a sprinkle of salt.

"What do you think?"

"I don't know. Have you come up with a name yet?"

"How about calling it a Saint Crusty?"

"Perfect! When is Saint Crusty going to be cooked?"

"Soon as she's been singed around the edges, I'll pull her out of the fire" I laughed.

Mixing and kneading a ball of dough and making a pie only requires patience and a bit of experience. Cooking a pie with moist ingredients in a frying pan on a galley stove requires a very delicate touch. Wendy and I often spent weeks and weeks in remote anchorages without resupplying. If we could manage to keep the weevils out of the flour, then I could always make an impromptu frying pan pie in minutes. A pie can be filled with practically anything. It is a terrific recipe staple that is normally edible. A vegetarian pie is simple. Cooking on a small galley stove is the hard part. Small marine stoves are rudimentary pieces of equipment that are one culinary step above a Hasbro Easy-Bake oven. If the frying pan becomes too hot when you are cooking a pie, the dough will cook too fast. It may have an attractive golden exterior with an uncooked and doughy interior. If it is cooked too slow the crust may look equally attractive but the crust will be tough as cardboard and the ingredients uncooked. There is absolutely no way of establishing a standardized cooking time and temperature for every type of pie. There are too many possibilities. The only instruments that are accurate enough to guarantee even the possibility of success are the nose, eyes and a good probe thermometer.

I placed the lidded frying pan on a medium low flame. After a few minutes I opened the lid for a smell. The only thing that should be smelled at this point is the gentle aroma of olive oil. I carefully ran a spatula under the pie. The edge and the bottom was just beginning to turn a light tan. I turned up the gas slightly to high medium. In five minutes I began to smell the dough. The bottom of the crust was now beginning to brown. This was a good time to practice attentiveness. I waited patiently then lifted the lid. The cheesy smell of the curds mixed with the sweet smell of the carrots and the vinegar of the pickled jalapeños was apparent. When you can smell the ingredients, they are beginning to merge. It was time to flip the pie. I placed a large dinner plate over the pan and flipped the pan over. The pie dropped out onto the plate then was slid bottom side up back into the pan. I cooked it for five minutes on medium low then pushed it to the back of the stove. After another five minutes of rest, I inserted the cooking thermometer. The reading was a proper 180° F.

A galley pie can be very tasty by itself, especially if it is made with a stronger cheese like Blue or Stilton. However, a milder pie can benefit from a good sauce that will give character and a bit of zip.

"How about a balsamic glaze?" I said to Wendy who was watching over my shoulder.

"Well, we've got carrots, raisins, pickled jalapeños, cottage cheese and potato. How about something sweet?"

"Maybe something sweet, hot and savory" I said.

"Like what?" Wendy asked.

"We still have a small bit of honey. Get that out. And get the balsamic vinegar too." Pulling the small sauce pan back out of the sink I placed it on the stove and turned on the burner. "There isn't much left in the bottles. Pour it all in and stir it with this" I said handing Wendy a tablespoon.

When the honey and the balsamic vinegar began to simmer I added cayenne pepper, a dot of cinnamon and a splash of aged rum.

"How long does it cook?" Wendy asked.

"Not cooking, reducing. Reduce it until it coats the back of the spoon. Keep going, you're close" I said. The sauce reduced in about four minutes. "OK, you can stop now" I said. "See how thick and glossy the sauce is getting?"

"Not really" Wendy said.

"Dip the back of the spoon in the sauce and hold it over the pot. See how the sauce drips? That's it. It's reduced. If you go any further it will turn into toffee. Get a platter and I'll plate up the pie."

Wendy reached into the cabinet and selected our fanciest platter. The pie was still warm. I slid it onto a cutting board and sliced it into one inch strips. While I drizzled the glaze over the crust, Wendy set the cockpit table.

"It looks great" she said looking down into the galley.

"Have a taste" I said proudly holding up a small piece.

"Wow, it tastes nothing like I expected" she said smiling.

"We make a great couple. You like everything I cook" I said laughing.

Wendy had dressed the cockpit table very nicely with a red checkered tablecloth. The flickering votive candle at each end gave the table the look of a primitive altar.

"This is pretty spiritual" I said carrying the pie up the cockpit stairs. "What's the occasion?"

"This is in honor of Saint Crusty, the Patron Saint of Pirates" Wendy laughed.

I lifted my glass of wine. "May Saint Crusty always sustain us" I said clinking glasses with Wendy. I picked up a piece of the pie and spread a tiny bit more glaze on it. "Not bad. A little butter in the dough would have made it richer. What a time to run out of butter."

"Why's that?" Wendy asked.

"We're in France, don't forget. A chef can get five years to life for faking butter with drained cottage cheese. It's a lot worse than showing up at Customs with phony boat documentation" I laughed.

When Saint Crusty was done, Wendy slid around to the port cushions and put her head in my lap.

"This is a really special place" I said looking around at the blue water and the crescent of beach that perfectly framed the hills of Îles des Saintes. "Do you hear that?" I said.

"What?"

"An outboard. It sounds so close" I said looking around. I picked up the binoculars and swept them across

163

the horizon. "I don't see anything. I think they might be on the other side of the island. Whoever it is, they're coming fast" I said.

We only had time to take a small sip of Chardonnay before a thirty foot, two engine pirogue sped into the harbor. A small, old, grizzled nervous man sat on the forward seat of the pirogue. A younger, more nervous captain was standing at the stern with the engine throttle in his hand. He made a wide high speed turn into the anchorage then cut the engine. A large wake caught up to the pirogue tossing it from side to side. The captain held onto the gunnels as the boat rocked. His eyes darted around the anchorage suspiciously.

"What's up with those two? They look like the devil's chasing them" I said.

The captain put a pair of binoculars to his eyes.

"What's he doing?" Wendy said.

"I'm not sure. He's looking around the back of the island. He's jumpy as a cat. Here they come" I said.

The captain dropped the binoculars in the bottom of the boat and gunned his engine.

"He's in a big hurry and he's coming right for us" I said reaching into the cockpit locker and pulling out the baseball bat.

His boat made a fast sweeping turn and swung around our stern, then slowed to a crawl. The smiling captain motored slowly up along side Quest.

"Hold onto this" I said handing Wendy the bat.

He grabbed onto Quest's gunnel and gave me a toothy smile. The pirogue was conspicuously overloaded

164

with crates of wine.

"Mon ami" he said reaching out with both hands.

"What?" I said.

"David. We've got another problem" Wendy said.

I turned around to see a French Police patrol boat heading straight for us with the blue lights flashing and the siren whaling.

"Please Monsieur" the smuggler pleaded as he grabbed onto Quest's gunnels and started to pull himself on board.

I caught him in the chest with the heel of my foot pushing him back into the pirogue.

"I don't forget this!" he said climbing over the crates of wine to reach the stern of his boat.

He grabbed the tiller and raced off. The crew of the patrol boat spotted him pulling away from our stern and took off after him.

"More problems!" Wendy shouted pointing to a second French patrol boat that was bearing down on us.

The official pulled along side. "Papers" he demanded.

"We're from Florida" I said.

He shrugged. "Have you checked in?"

"We just got in five minutes ago" I said.

He looked suspiciously at the empty plates and the bottle of wine on the table. "Five minutes?" he said pointing his finger at me. "Check in tomorrow. I'll be back."

Sixteen

Sugar Rush

"I don't think we want to be around when he shows up tomorrow" I said.

"Who, the wine smuggler or the cop?" Wendy asked grinning.

"Forget about the smuggler. He's '*sans bateau, sans vin*' right about now" I said pouring the last sip of the Chardonnay. "As for the cop. Let's consider ourselves lucky. We'll book out of here at sunrise tomorrow."

"I couldn't agree more" Wendy said.

When the dishes were cleared away we settled in to the forward berth for a good sleep.

I was suddenly pulled out of a vivid dream the next morning by a flock of seagulls noisily feeding on a school of small fish just off our transom. They swept in low erratic circles over the glassy silver blue surface of the motionless anchorage. A sliver of sun had just popped over the low hills of Terre-de-Haut. The gulls' bright white feathers reflected the orange morning light and the phosphorescent blues of the water. Driven by the forces of instinct and need, they made coordinated dives at the surface, forcing the school of fish to leap into the air. The

Sugar Rush

preoccupied flock of fowl paid no attention as I started the
engine and prepared Quest for sail. Wendy stood in the
companionway, stretched, yawned and looked at the
squawking gulls.

"What are they eating for breakfast?" she asked
pointing to the seagull feeding frenzy.

"All you can eat fish fry" I replied walking to the
bow and hauling up the anchor.

With the anchor up and Quest heading away from
the beach, the short voyage to the northern Dominican city
of Portsmouth was underway. We had twenty miles of easy
sailing before us. When we had cleared Pointe Boisjolie, I
steered south towards the reef strewn channel between
Grand Îlet and the very small island of La Coche. With
these two islands cleared, I raised the sails and we settled
into the rhythm of a steady trade wind and a gentle swell.

Dominica is the first island that Columbus
discovered on his second voyage to the Caribbean in 1493
but it has been the last to share in the wealth of the
Caribbean. As the most mountainous island of the Lesser
Antilles, Dominica's towering volcanic landscape and
diverse permanent rain forest create a dense and almost
impregnable mysterious tropical world. The farming of
bananas and pineapples is the industry that sustains the
island's meager economy.

Prince Rupert's Bay on the northwest corner of
Dominica is an all weather anchorage. It is well protected
from the constant assault of the trade winds. Prince
Rupert's Bay provides a welcome haven to cruisers calling
in from all over the world. The effortless twenty mile sail

167

between Îles des Saintes and Portsmouth seemed to be over in minutes. We rounded the high solo volcano standing sentinel in Cabrits National Park at the northern extremity of the Bay and found plenty of room. There was good holding one hundred feet from shore directly in front of the Purple Turtle Restaurant.

Our 10:00 arrival gave us ample time to check in at Customs and resupply before lunch.

"So where's Customs?" I asked Wendy as we sped south in the anchorage.

"It's in front of the government dock. That big dock" Wendy said pointing a mile south up the beach.

I slowed down and motored through a small cluster of fishing pirogues before pulling beside the stark concrete dock.

"Can we leave our boat here?" I asked a policeman that was strolling the deserted dock.

"Leave it right dere. It be safe. If you look for Customs, it dere" he said pointing to a rough gray building across a dusty narrow road.

We crossed Moo Cow Lane and opened the front door of Customs, stepping out of the hot tropical sun into a sparsely lighted room that was hotter and steamier than the surrounding jungle.

"I don't see anybody. Do you think we should come back later?" Wendy said looking around the vacant office.

"Let's wait a couple minutes" I said. When my eyes had adjusted to the light I saw the only vivid display of color in the drab room. "Hey, look at that mango" I said pointing to the end of the counter.

Sugar Rush

Walking over I picked up the ripe mango and smelled it.

"Keep your hands off my Julie mango."

I swiveled around to see a six foot three Customs officer decked out in a brand new, crisply starched uniform. His angry frown turned into an inviting grin.

"I just kidding mon. I Tommy" he said extending his hand. "Ever had a Julie mango?" he asked.

"What's a Julie mango?" I said.

He pulled a plate and a knife from under the counter and cut up the mango into wedges.

"Try dis" he said passing the plate to Wendy.

The intoxicating tropical fragrance filled the room. Wendy ate a piece and smiled.

"This is really good. It tastes like mango custard" she said.

He passed me the plate. "Dis from sister's tree. It hybrid, dis no bush mango." He pulled out a local map of Plymouth and showed us where to find the fruit market. "Now your papers" he said trying to sound official.

I snapped the passports out of my shirt pocket. He opened them up to the Montserrat stamp.

"What dis?" he said pointing to the stamps. "Dis say you two check out Montserrat four days ago. Why it take you four days to sail from Little Bay?"

I was not ready with an appropriately evasive answer. "We stopped in Guadeloupe."

He leafed through the passport. "Where Guadeloupe stamp?" he asked.

I began to offer a plausible answer when he waved a

169

dismissive hand over the passport.

"Deshaies Customs, bunch o' clowns. My cousin, he be officer in Deshaies. He never in office. Always in cafe. Good job eh?" he said laughing. He reached over and inked our arrival and departure stamps. "Wait a minute" he said as I turned to leave. "Here, have a good Dominica Julie mango" he said reaching into a paper bag.

On the other side of Moo Cow Lane, the police officer was still standing on the dock above our dinghy.

"I watch your dinghy" the officer said touching the dinghy painter. "Many thieves here."

This implication of deserved baksheesh needed addressing.

"You like mangoes?" I asked the officer. He looked at me with utter contempt. "It's a Julie mango" I said enthusiastically.

"Julie mango. OK, sure mon."

The policeman reached down and took the mango. With a push from the officer's boot, he sent us on our way with a fresh black streak on the Porta-Bote's top side. When we had motored halfway to the city dock Wendy turned around.

"You gave away my Julie mango" she said with a frown.

"I'll buy you a bucket of Julie mangoes" I said holding up the bailing bucket.

Beaching the dinghy on a low sandy bluff, we passed between two weathered and worn shacks to find ourselves on Bay Street, the major thoroughfare of the village. Portsmouth has been continuously settled for over three hundred years. It is the second largest city on the island with a population of only 3000 souls. The mean, small, weathered wooden shacks and two story crumbling concrete structures spoke of many years of chronic poverty. In spite of their modest circumstances the people of Portsmouth were radiant with good will. Everyone that passed by greeted us with smiles.

One block up the street we spotted the overflowing tables of the fruit market clustered in the shade of a breadfruit tree. We were greeted by the first stall vendor.

"Got anything sweet for me today?" I said to the old woman.

She casually waved flies away with her straw hat and smiled. "Sweeter than pineapple?" she asked.

"We'll take two of your ripest pineapples. Do you have any Julie mangoes?" I asked.

"So, how do you know Julie Mango?" she said, sliding a cardboard box from under the stall.

"Tommy at Customs introduced us" I said.

"Dese better than his sister's mango" she said placing about ten mangoes in Wendy's cloth bag.

"Don't forget those big sweet pineapples" I said. She held out one for me to smell. "Good" I said.

"Dat be four dollars" she said smiling.

While Wendy paid and chatted with Grandma I looked around at the decaying urban landscape of rusty tin roofs, weathered clapboard houses, muddy streets and happy people. My eyes strayed to the wide gap between two dilapidated beach shacks which gave an unobstructed view of Prince Rupert's Bay and the million dollar fleet of cruising sailboats bobbing at anchor. 'Poverty and wealth, wealth and poverty, what an inappropriate place for me to be looking for paradise' I thought as we walked between the shacks to the dinghy on the beach. Children chased each other around stubbly front yards. Grandmothers sat with daughters on small porches peeling vegetables, braiding hair, talking and laughing. I glanced up to one of the porches and said good morning to the group of women. I felt less of an intruder when I heard the mingled voices of their warm welcome.

"Why don't we sail down to Roseau tomorrow?" I said hefting the weighty, fruity bag of mangoes and pineapples onto Quest's foredeck.

"We do need to keep moving. And we won't need anymore pineapple" Wendy agreed.

"Peel three of the mangoes. I'll core this pineapple. We'll have a fruit salad sugar blast for lunch" I said rubbing the edge of a heavy kitchen knife with a honing steel.

The cored and peeled pineapple was sliced into bite size pieces. The fragrant tropical aroma that filled the cabin was overpowering. The pineapple was mixed in a bowl with the sliced mangoes, a teaspoon of rum, a teaspoon of vanilla and a splash of orange juice for acidity. The bright yellow color of the pineapple blended perfectly with the deep orange of the mango.

"Ready for a sugar rush?" I said carrying the bowl up the companionway.

I gorged on mango and pineapple until my stomach felt like it was ready to burst. With about half a pound of sugar in my belly, I laid down in the heat of the cockpit and perspired pure fructose.

In the morning most of my sugar tremors had worn off. We would make the short sail south to Roseau, the capitol of Dominica. The anchor was raised while the air was cool and musky from the tropical jungle. We motored three miles due west out of the lee of Dominica to catch a light trade wind that carried us to Roseau on a strong beam reach. The sparsely populated high mountains and thick tropical forests give the western coast of Dominica a wild primitive appearance. The rugged mountain peaks seem to drop out of the clouds and descend precipitously to the blue Caribbean. Innumerable shady valleys add mystery to the craggy hills that plunge straight past the shoreline to incredible underwater depths.

We dropped the sails a short distance south of Roseau and motored in close to shore. I began sounding off the community of Castle Comfort.

"This is unbelievable. There's no bottom. I think we're going to touch shore before the depth gauge comes off infinite" I said to Wendy.

I carefully nudged Quest's bow to within ten feet of the shore. I backed up and tried a number of times further up the shore before giving up.

"We'll have to drop, back to shore then tie off to a palm tree" I was saying to Wendy when we heard the VHF radio crackle to life.

"Dis Rocky, you in wrong place to anchor. You pick up my mooring. It tree hundred feet south. I be there now. I wait" he said.

I looked south. A very tall Rastafarian in a half

sunken pirogue was waving his arms in the air thirty feet from shore.

"How much for the mooring?" I asked over the radio.

"Twenty-five US dollars."

"Forget it" I said.

"You not charter boat?" he asked.

"NO" I said emphatically.

"That charter boat price. Only five dollar for cruiser" he said.

I motored the short distance to where Rocky stood in a pirogue that was leaking faster than he could bail.

"I Rocky" he said reaching over the gunnels to shake my hand. "Nice to meet you."

"Five bucks" I said.

"Five bucks a day and for twenty, I'll carry you to grocery store in Roseau in minivan."

"We'll walk to Roseau" I said.

"No. Roseau too far, mon" he said.

"OK, ten dollars for the round trip" I said taking the mooring pendant.

"Hurry fast mon, boat sinking" he said frantically throwing buckets of water over the side.

Wendy and I had slipped into the cabin to put on shoes when we heard Rocky climbing on deck. He appeared at the companionway and smiled down at us with a sheepish grin.

"Boat gone."

"What?" I said.

"Boat sunk. Not to worry. I dive down and get boat

174

tomorrow" he said confidently.

"How long has it been leaking?"

"I don't know mon. Not my boat."

All three of us climbed down into our dinghy.

"This dinghy very ugly boat" he said insulting our Porta-Bote on the ride to shore.

"It's above water" I said sharply.

"Yes mon" he said reaching over the side and squeezing out his long water sodden dreadlocks.

We beached and tied off the dinghy to a palm while Rocky brought the van to the beach.

"Nice van" I said as he opened the doors. "Own it long?"

"Dis my boss van. It mine now. He out of town every Thursday. Where we go?" he asked.

"Just downtown to the supermarket" I said.

Rocky couldn't drive and talk at the same time. The three mile trip to the supermarket took over an hour and included a detailed historic tour of every street in the delightful and prosperous city of Roseau.

"I wait in shade" he said pulling up in front of the Chinese grocery store.

The wide ranging, eclectic mix of merchandise inside the store gave it the aura of a Chinese bazaar. 'If we don't have it, you don't need it' read a large black-on-white sign tacked to the back wall. If you needed a tire iron, Buddhist gong, chop sticks, incense burners, shampoo, motor scooter, wheel barrow, cheap rum or champagne, they had it. We filled up a basket of fresh vegetables and a selection of dairy products.

"Do you want more pineapple?" Wendy asked.

"No. My heart is still doing the sugar flutter from yesterday."

We paid, and at the insistence of the owner, a young man carried our packages out to the curb.

"There's Rocky" Wendy said.

The van was a block down the street under a tree.

"How's it going Rocky?" I said when we reached the van with our groceries.

He was lounging in the back seat with a very large spliff between his fingers.

"Want a toke mon?"

"Not right now. Bones and boats don't mix" I said.

Rocky shrugged and squeezed into the front seat. The van screeched away from the curb before we had a chance to pull the back doors shut. A block down the street, Rocky had to stop for congested traffic.

"This traffic too much. Nobody know how to drive 'round here" he said pulling over the curb onto the sidewalk then turning the wrong way on a one way street.

"This is the wrong way" Wendy yelled.

"Don't worry bout it. Dat sign always wrong."

He successfully weaved his way in and out of traffic until we were safely out of town.

"There's our dinghy" I said.

He slammed on the brakes. The van slid to a halt on the sand slicked road.

"Wanna party?" he asked.

"No" I said.

"Not you mon. I talking to her."

Seventeen

Dust from Africa

Having the opportunity to be responsible for a boat and her crew on the big ocean will most certainly provide a captain with innumerable lessons on the advantages of being attentive. Among the most valuable of these lessons is that no decision while at sea is inconsequential. Procrastination is an inappropriate luxury that is best left on shore. Sailing is a solitary occupation where action not only defines who you are, but also who you will become.

I found an unexpected surprise waiting for me when we climbed aboard Quest to stow our purchases from Roseau. As I set the bag of groceries on the saloon table I heard the customary scratchy and repetitive sound of the single side band radio downloading a weather fax to the laptop. The hurricane season was well under way. Downloading and analyzing daily weather updates was routine. In the last few weeks, the tropical waves that trundle their way across the Atlantic from Sub-Saharan Africa had become stronger and more frequent. Atmospheric low pressure troughs, or tropical waves as they are known in the Caribbean, are weather events similar to an enormous squall line hundreds of miles long that are always oriented north to south. These atmospheric troughs are created by high pressure systems over the Azores and appear as an arching black line on a weather fax. Most Caribbean hurricanes are spawned from tropical waves after they pick up momentum in the mid Atlantic. Before they become cyclonic, a tropical wave is not a particularly dangerous weather event, unless you are in a deep roadstead that becomes untenable with every storm.

The sight of this very large tropical wave heading in our direction was unsettling. This was a banner year for wave activity. A constant crop of tropical waves had blown through the Caribbean each week with exceptional regularity. The leading edge of each wave brought stronger, gale force winds and torrential rain. This approaching tropical wave had exceptional strength and was predicted to have cyclonic activity.

Roseau is only a moderately good fair weather roadstead. The very high mountain range in the interior of Dominica provides protection from wind. This harbor provides no protection from ocean surge. What concerned me more was Rocky's a*d hoc* mooring. If it didn't hold up to the stress of a hard surge it could break and we would be on the beach before we had time to react.

"We're going to have to get out of Roseau soon."

"What's going on?" Wendy said looking over my shoulder at the screen.

"This is what's going on" I said pointing to the long arch of the tropical wave. "The storm may not be too bad but we're in the wrong place on a kludgey Rastified mooring. We might be able to find a quiet place in Martinique."

"No way, I don't want to push our luck with French Customs again. What's choice number two?" Wendy asked.

"Rodney Bay on St. Lucia. It's about ninety miles. If we leave at sundown we'll be there by noon tomorrow" I said opening the spreaders and laying the points on the chart. "Help me get the dinghy lashed and sails prepped. Then we can make a quick getaway. First we should get a couple of hours rest."

It seemed I had no sooner laid down when the alarm went off. I opened my eyes. An orange, slanted ray of afternoon sun shot through the porthole and illuminated the teak wall.

I slapped my hands together hard and said "It's time to get up."

"I'm already awake" Wendy said taking the towel off her eyes.

Jumping down from the berth I walked to the galley and filled a sauce pan with two cups of fresh water. I tightened the pan hard in the fiddles and started the flame. When the water began to boil, I added a cup of rinsed Basmati rice and a pinch of salt.

"Hey, what are you cooking?" Wendy asked from the forward berth.

"I thought this might bring you around. It's some rice for a midnight snack" I said.

Climbing the companionway I switched on the engine, went forward and threw the seaweed-covered mooring pendant into the water with a sodden splash. The golden sun dipped low to the horizon as we motored the five miles to the southern tip of Dominica. The jib and mainsail filled with a reassuring crisp snap. We cleared the Scott's Head shallows and caught a strong fresh breeze. Quest leaped forward at a comfortable six knots with a foaming white wave curling at her bow. Behind us the vibrant tropical vegetation that blankets Dominica slowly turned from green to deep purple and then to black as the setting sun finally touched the horizon sending bands of orange light streaking into the sky.

When we had sailed out of the lee of Dominica I dropped into the cabin to take a close look at the more recent afternoon weather fax. The tropical wave had made an unexpected rapid advance. The predicted wind at the front of the wave was thirty five knots blowing almost due west. The leading edge would hit us a little after midnight. I was still optimistic that we could outrun the storm.

"Look at the chart" I said to Wendy. "We should be able to stay in the lee of Martinique when the leading edge hits. We're going to get some wind, but the sea shouldn't be too bad. I'll take the first watch and wake you at twelve o'clock.

"OK" Wendy said walking forward to the berth.

The wind held steady at fifteen knots with a mild sea. I drifted in and out of light sleep with the squeak of the autopilot invading my dreams. When the alarm clock woke me at midnight, I groped for the light switch before checking our position on the GPS. We had put about half our trip behind us. Judging by the smell and the bright lights of the garbage fires on shore we were solidly in the lee of Martinique. The faint acrid smell of burning plastic wafted into the cockpit with every shifting gust of wind.

"Wake up, Wendy. You've got to see this" I called down into the cabin.

"OK, I'll be right there. What's that stink? Did you burn something?" she called back.

"Check this out. Look at all the fires on Martinique" I said.

"What are they, beach fires?"

"No, that's what I thought before I smelled the smoke. Take these" I said handing her the binoculars. "I'm pretty sure they're very big garbage fires."

"They smell pretty bad, but they still look pretty cool. Hey, something's happening over there. They all just got a lot brighter" Wendy said looking through the binoculars.

"They are getting brighter, but why are all of them getting brighter at the same time?" I said.

"See for yourself" she said handing me the binoculars.

"It looks like the wind just picked up and it's fanning the flames" I said. Then I looked above the island. "Wait a minute, look at that long cloud over Martinique. It's stretching all the way across the horizon and it's moving very fast."

The flames of each individual garbage fire continued to flare up until they were a brilliant white. Then in an instant, as if a switch were thrown, they all went out exactly at the same time. Thirty miles of coastline disappeared into darkness.

"It's rain" I said. "The rain at the leading edge of the storm must have put out all of the fires. I bet we're going to get hit by the same squall line in less than ten minutes. Let's move fast" I said frantically furling in the jib and easing out the staysail.

Very large raindrops began to plink off the mainsail and hardtop seconds before becaming a constant drumming.

"Hold on" I said as the first gale force gusts of wind caught the main.

A high pitched vibration screamed through the rigging as we heeled to starboard. Then an even more intense blast hit us that sent the starboard rail slowly under water. I struggled to my feet and let the mainsheet out further. Quest responded and came out of her heel.

"Look behind us" Wendy yelled over the roar of the wind.

I turned on the stern spot light. Line upon line of white breakers rushed at our stern out of the darkness. We both involuntarily ducked as a boarding wave broke and slammed against the dinghy.

"Where did that come from?"

"Well I guess that we aren't quite in the lee of Martinique" Wendy said.

"You should see it on the other side of Martinique. Check our course Wendy."

"We're within two degrees" she shouted back.

I looked behind us at another wall of white foam surging under the stern. "What's our speed?"

"Seven knots" she said.

"That's impossible. Look again" I said.

"It's seven point five and getting faster!" she said as another breaking wave skewed Quest's stern to port like a toy.

'What a time to set a speed record' I thought. "This speed is helping a lot" I shouted optimistically.

"Why?" Wendy shouted back dubiously.

"If we can almost keep up to these waves, it's going to be a lot more comfortable."

This little nugget of wisdom seemed more like hopefulness than reality as another breaker loomed up behind us. Wave after wave slammed against the transom with a crashing roar. In a following sea, if the speed of the waves slapping at your stern move faster than your boat, they will overtake you. They will then pass the length of the boat from stern to bow. Sailing in a following sea at night is strangely unsettling. In the darkness with only the waves and the boat as reference, one gets the strange sensation of traveling backwards.

Getting comfortable steering in a following sea took a few minutes of practice and a great deal of upper body strength and agility. Before long I could feel when the next wave was about to lift the stern. As her stern began to rise, the tremendous pressure of the water pushed Quest's transom sideways. A quarter turn on the wheel and the rudder brought her back in line. Then fifteen seconds later the transom would seem to drop out from underneath me. The hissing, white-capped wave traveled forward along the length of the hull, shipping water over the gunnels and deck.

Quest in the Caribbean

The worst of the storm was over in two hours. I was more than ready for the wind to lighten and the waves return to a quartering sea. I looked over my shoulder into the eastern sky. The excitement of the brief storm faded as fatigue began to overtake me. Our heading was good. There was no longer any reason to finesse the steering. I let the jib out then reached over the pedestal and engaged the autopilot. Leaning back into the cockpit cushions, I pulled the windbreaker over my shoulders and fell into a sound sleep.

"What's going on here?" Wendy said standing over me. "I can't leave you at the wheel for ten minutes" she laughed.

"Did you heat up the rice?" I asked.

"Coming right up" she said dropping into the galley.

I stood up and stretched. The sun was a few degrees above the horizon. The black edge of the tropical wave was a fast disappearing line on the western horizon. An expansive crystal blue sky spread out in its wake. There was a fresh sweetness to the air. The rain-rinsed brightwork and stainless sparkled in the morning light. Drops of water glistened and flashed like jewel rainbows as they flew from the edge of the billowing main.

Looking over the flatlands of nothern St. Lucia, the mist-shrouded magnificent peak of Mount Gimie looked like a postcard.

"Here's your hot buttered rice" Wendy said handing me a bowl and sitting beside me. "What a night" she said.

"What a night is right" I agreed.

"I remember you telling me that we were going to

stay in the lee of Martinique. What happened?"

"Reality happened. Or when you're dealing with big islands, big storms, big currents and who knows what else, who can predict? It could have been a lot worse. We could have been sailing the other direction. Hand me the St. Lucia chart with the Rodney Bay insert" I said.

Pigeon Island National Park is a long peninsula of land that forms the northern extremity of delightfully immense Rodney Bay. The bay can accommodate thousands of sailboats. The dredged Rodney Bay Marina lagoon, ½ mile south, is one of the best hurricane holes in the Caribbean with hundreds of docks. It wasn't until we rounded the corner of Pigeon Island National Park and came into Rodney Bay that I realized the scale of development on St. Lucia. Stretching out before us was a mile and a half of upscale resorts. The red tiled hotel roofs stretched along the white sand beach from one end of the bay to the other. The developers had not yet usurped the right to anchor in the harbor.

Scanning the northern half of the anchorage I found a likely anchoring spot just off the Sandals all-you-can-eat resort.

"Wait a minute" I said. "Steer a little further north. I think I see something."

Wendy brought the bow around.

"Hey guess what? It looks like Joe and Patrice made it to Rodney Bay. They're right over there, behind that catamaran" I said.

"I see them" Wendy said.

Walking to the bow I pulled the safety pin on the

185

anchor and slipped the brake handle on the windlass. Wendy pulled about one hundred feet in front of Amethyst and I dropped the anchor and one hundred feet of chain. Quest fell back in the strong breeze and snubbed down hard.

"Joe and Patrice must be on shore" I said to Wendy while I covered the main sail.

I was just wondering how they had made out with their sail repair when I heard the sound of a small outboard and turned around. Joe pulled along side, stopped his engine and held onto the gunnels.

"How's everything?" he said with a smile and a shake of my hand.

"Good, we just came in."

"Have a good night sail?" he asked.

"Very exciting night sail" I replied.

"Yeah, it even got a bit rough in the anchorage last night when the squall blew through" he said.

"So what happened with your sail? Can they fix it?"

"That sail is a write-off. The guy at the loft said it's too worn out to repair. We've ordered an off-the-rack cruising sail from Doyle. It's definitely going to be here tomorrow or maybe the next day or next week" he said rolling his eyes.

"If you need some help putting it up, come and get us."

"Will do" he said pushing off.

"Hey Joe" I said calling him back. "What's with all this haze in the air? The sun was blood red this morning. I thought it might be all the open pit garbage fires on

186

Martinique" I said.

Joe smiled. "No, this is definitely not Martinique garbage fires. I just ran into a guy in the marina that was chartering a work boat for a couple of days. He's an atmospheric scientist from France and he's been studying on Martinique for most of the summer. You're going to laugh. When I told him that I've been cleaning red dust off the decks since we got to Rodney Bay, he said 'Of course you've been cleaning up red dust. What did you expect? Sand's been blowing across the Atlantic for the last 20 million years. This is dust from Africa, mon ami'."

Eighteen

Rich mon poor

I woke up only a stone's throw away from the pinnacle of Caribbean luxury. Pulling on my favorite old t-shirt I began another beautiful, do it yourself day in paradise. Wendy was also working hard. She was leaning against a cockpit cushion and swaying to the gentle rhythm of the ocean with a hot cup of tea in her hand.

"A spot of Earl Grey?" she said smiling.

"Yes" I said clearing my dry throat. "How's our African real estate today?" I asked.

Wendy looked at me blankly. "What?"

"The African dust?"

"Oh, the dust, look around the scupper" Wendy said pointing to the forward combing.

Reaching down I took a pinch between my fingers. "This looks like genuine dirt. I'll be right back" I said going to the cabin for a piece of printer paper and the scope. I laid the paper on the cockpit table and sprinkled the dust in the center.

"It doesn't look very red" Wendy said.

I bent down and looked through a 15x scope. Wetting the tip of a finger I ran it through the little pile of dust. It left a brown-red streak down the center of the page.

"What do you know? It is red. You just have to add spit" I said.

"Do you think it's really from Africa?" Wendy asked.

"Unless it a cheap imported knockoff, it's from North Africa" I laughed.

Wendy stood up and threw the last dregs of her tea overboard. "When are we going to check in?" she asked

"Right now" I said turning around and lowering the dinghy from the davits.

The light, warm, dry morning air barely ruffled the surface of the anchorage. We glided our way south along the shore passing billions of dollars worth of resort properties until we entered the dredged canal leading to the Rodney Bay Marina lagoon.

The how's and why's of wealth distribution on Caribbean islands is no less obfuscating than any other place in the world. Dominica's economy sputters along on the exportation of bananas and pineapples. Only one hundred miles south, St. Lucia's economy shines with the glitter of a million diamonds. Both countries are equally dressed in natural finery and outstanding tropical beauty. Each country has similar colonial origins. St. Lucia and Dominica are populated by an almost identical ethnic makeup. Their forms of governance are similar, stable democracies. Aside from these basic attributes, their economies are complete opposites.

What regions or countries of the world don't strive

to earn economic independence and wealth? Everyone wants to be successful, don't they? In the normal course of events, states accrue wealth over time by investment and industry while exploiting regional advantage. In the 1850's coal fields, iron ore, and canals gave birth to the steel industry in America and Europe. Even in prehistoric time, mankind harnessed the raw power of nature to fabricate the perceived needs of an eager consumer. Today industry can survive in places once believed to be manufacturing deserts. For three hundred years the western world held great hope for Caribbean colonization. With the economic advantage of slavery, Europeans dreamed of an agricultural utopia in the West Indies that would feed the world and fill their pockets. The slaves are emancipated but bananas still sell for ten cents a pound.

All islands in the Caribbean have dreamed of ditching the banana and mango agrarian model for the more uptown, sleek and sexy model of modern Caribbean privateering. The quickest pathway to wealth in the Caribbean is to ditch the fruit and jump into international banking with both feet. The only thing necessary is for the islands' governing bodies to sign the paperwork and the gold begins to flow. St. Lucia is triply blessed. Along with a thriving banking sector, tropical sun, and a few sandy beaches they have one thing that most of the other Caribbean islands lack: a few thousand acres of flat land that make developers drool. The vast majority of the beautiful, volcanic terrain of St. Lucia is too mountainous to grow pineapples. One notable exception to all of the hilly terrain in the Lesser Antilles is the top third of St.

Lucia. It may be no bigger than Manhattan but it is big enough and flat enough to graze a herd of voracious developers.

As we motored through the inner lagoon of Rodney Bay Marina, the fleets of a half dozen charter companies lay mothballed, their decks baking in the summer sun waiting out hurricane season. The Rodney Bay Marina has a plentiful array of yacht servicing businesses which crowd the two story buildings along the breakwall at the head of the marina.

"So where do you think Customs is?" I asked Wendy as we stepped up unto the dock.

Wendy thumbed through the guide. "There it is" she said pointing to a door on the upper floor.

I stole a quick glance through the door of the yacht charter welcome center as I walked by. After passing Louis' Authentic Parisian Breads and Hans' Certified European Cheeses, we climbed the stairs. Finding the door to Customs open, we entered the brightly lit office.

The officer stood motionless at the counter reading the St. Lucia Times. Without looking up from the newspaper, he pulled a form down from a hanging rack and clicked his pen. "What charter company are you with?"

I looked at Wendy, then back at the officer. "We're not with a charter company."

"The bathroom is two doors down and to the right" he said sliding the immigration form back into its slot.

"I'm the captain of the sailing vessel Quest. We came in yesterday" I said.

He looked up with little interest. "Ah, what?" he said.

"I want to check in."

"Why didn't you say that when you came in?" he said folding the newspaper. "You said you came in yesterday? When yesterday?" he asked poised with pen in hand.

I looked down at the floor. "Late yesterday."

"How late?" he insisted.

"Late yesterday morning. Maybe around ten."

"Well you're twenty-four hours late, Quest. You're playing very loose with St. Lucia Customs, don't you think?"

"Right you are" I said smiling.

With an irritated expression on his face he snatched the passports from my hand. "You get two weeks."

I picked up the passports and walked quietly onto the balcony. A young man in a Moorings Charters windbreaker passed us on the stairs.

"Watch yourself" I said to him as he approached the Customs door.

"Watch what?" he said.

"The Customs dude isn't in a good mood" I said.

"Oh, what charter company you with? I'll have them have a talk with the officer."

"We're cruisers" I said.

"Aha" he said stepping back from the two pariahs. "Can't help you then."

"I don't need any help."

"Here's the thing" he said. "You're in charter

country. That office is bought and paid for by my company. Maybe you should know the lay of the land before you go making comments."

Wendy and I eyed each other and I broke out laughing.

"What's the big joke?" he said as we turned and started down the stairs.

I turned to Wendy and put my hand on her shoulder. Trying to hold back another laugh I said to her "What's it feel like to be a poor cruiser? That's one nice thing about being in Dominica two days ago. I was a rich man in Portsmouth. Today I'm a poor low life cruiser in Rodney Bay. Hey, let's go to the back door of the French cafe. Maybe they'll give us a stale crust of bread" I said to Wendy as we walked down the portico.

"A stale croissant sounds better" Wendy said opening the door of the cafe.

Joe and Patrice looked comfortable at a table near the counter. "Hey what a nice surprise seeing you two. Come and join us" Patrice said.

Wendy sat down while I carried a fourth chair from an adjoining table.

Joe looked at the passports in my shirt pocket. "Looks like you just came from Customs."

"Yeah, we just came from Happy Jacks two minutes ago."

Joe nodded. "Next time you go to Customs bring them some of these pastries" he said.

"How's your new jib coming along?" I asked.

"Same as yesterday. It's going to be here tomorrow" Joe laughed.

"How long are you two staying in Rodney Bay?" Patrice asked.

I looked at Wendy, then back at Patrice. "It's already late July. We should have been in Grenada a month ago" I said.

"I know what you mean. This has been a bad year for troughs. If our sails don't show up soon I think we're going to rent dock space for a few months and ride the hurricane season out with the charter boats. Why don't you and Wendy stay here? The marina has a great cruiser special. One space for the price of two while supplies last" Joe said.

"Thanks anyway. If we move fast we can be in Grenada before the end of the month" I said.

"So you two are going to be safe and sound below 12° while Joe and I have to fear the big, bad hurricane" Patrice said laughing.

"When are you leaving?" Joe asked.

"I think we'll be heading south tomorrow or the next day. The weather looks like it's going to hold for a while. I think we might go anchor in Marigot Bay."

Joe and Patrice gave each other side glances. "I'm not looking to change your mind, but Marigot Bay? It's very crowded this time of year. There are wall-to-wall charter boats. We rented a car yesterday and drove down. You might want to give the Pitons a try instead. It's twenty miles down the coast" Patrice said.

"We were there last year. It's probably going to be

more your style and it's going to be deserted this time of year" Joe said.

"OK, the Pitons it will be" I said setting my empty cup of tea down. "You two stay safe" I said as we left the cafe.

Wendy and I spent the rest of the morning wandering about the shops that cluster around the docks. There were more marine services in a half acre of property than I had ever seen in one place. The chandlers, sail lofts, grocery stores and book stores were doing a slow off season business. Over on the docks, six summer budget charterers proudly stood on the foredeck of their boats beaming with joy as two charter company employees explained anchoring basics.

We were happy and content to be headed back to the solitude of Quest for a late lunch and nap. We were getting into the dinghy when a very young boy dressed in only a pair of dirty, ragged pants ran out from from between two buildings shouting at us.

"I help you. I help you" he said smiling and taking Wendy's shopping bags. "I Abe. I carry every ting for you. Not charge much."

I shrugged and nodded. The young man took the two bags and placed them in the bottom of the dinghy with great care. Reaching in my pocket I gave him a twenty cent euro I'd found on the ground outside the cafe. He looked at the coin.

"Thanks mon. Now I come out to boat and wash dust off decks. I do real good job, only one euro."

I was just about to send him away when a marina

guard came running up swinging a night stick.

"Get out of here" he said giving Abe a shove.

"I got job. I works for dem" Abe said backing away from the guard with his hands raised.

"You don't work here. Don't come back" the guard said pointing the stick at Abe's chest.

As the young boy walked away with a disappointed look on his face the guard leaned over above the dinghy. "Don't give dem money anymore. It make dem bold."

"OK" I said starting the dinghy engine. I looked at Wendy when the guard was out of earshot. "Three days ago we were rich, this morning we were poor, and now we're back to being rich."

Fortunes are made and lost very fast in the Caribbean. I spun the dinghy around and turned into the channel.

A beautiful quiet evening was followed by a more beautiful dawn the next morning. A mild off shore breeze barely raised a ripple in the anchorage. It was the start of a perfect day for our twenty mile sail down to the Pitons. When I walked to the bow to winch up the anchor, I noticed a slight red-brown stain around the scuppers and thought of the dust that had traveled two thousand miles from Africa. The sound of the anchor chain rattling through the windlass carried over the water in the quiet stillness of the morning. Battalions of local workers swarmed about the resorts, raking seaweed from the beaches and precisely arranging umbrellas and chairs for the resort guests who would soon be awake and ready for an early morning nap in the warm tropical sun.

Rich mon poor

We left the bay with all sails drawing in the light air. We slowly picked up speed. Quest left an almost imperceptible wake as Rodney Bay disappeared behind us. It seemed as if we had just finished our bowls of cereal when we were forced to maneuver around two jumbo sized cruise ships making a morning call in the very large port of Castries. Two miles further south, the coastline indented to reveal the huge Hess Oil crude oil storage facility. A few minutes later the fjord shaped Marigot Bay came into view. Dozens of charter boats swung placidly at their summer moorings in turquoise water.

After Marigot Bay the coast line of St. Lucia becomes very rugged and sparsely inhabited. The flat land of the north island gives way to grand volcanic mountain peaks interspersed with dramatically inviting, mysterious shady valleys. The rich, warm earthy smells of the rain forest carried by a soft trade wind drifted down from the hills and out to sea. Watching the primitive wild landscape roll by mile after mile became blissfully hypnotic.

When we reached the peninsula of land that juts into the ocean just south of Anse Chastanet Beach, we swung seaward to avoid the reefs. After clearing this rocky point of land, we got our first unforgettable view of the Pitons. The Pitons are two enormous, comely shaped, volcanic mountain spires. Gros Piton and Petit Piton, both at around a half mile of elevation, each begin their practically vertical ascents right at the shore. These tremendous, bazooka-shaped peaks of almost unworldly dimensions dominate the landscape and seem to stand guard on each side of Piton Bay. The richly forested area

197

below the peaks is a World Heritage site covering 7200 acres of dark green forest and blue sea.

Piton Bay is extremely deep with practically no shelf. Trying to anchor is a lesson in futility. Anchoring at the head of the bay in front of the very upscale Viceroy Resort is a mistake that isn't easily overlooked by management. Our final destination for the morning was the tiny mooring field which lies along the shore, practically in the shadow of Gros Piton. We dropped sail and motored between the Pitons. The residual effect of the storm which had blown us from Dominica was raising a particularly nasty three foot ocean swell that slapped our stern as we entered the bay. As Quest rolled from side to side, I walked to the bow with the boat hook.

"OK, put her in neutral" I said.

Quest coasted twenty feet. I snagged the loop of the mooring pendant and pulled the pendant aboard.

Nineteen

Rastamen

After stowing the sails and giving the decks a good scrubbing we had nothing better to do than take a swim in the deep blue waters of Piton Bay. Warm sun and cool water was the perfect tonic following a day of coasting along St. Lucia. With little distraction, I soon fell asleep with my feet resting on the swim ladder. When the afternoon had grown long, the shadow cast by the enormous peak of Gros Piton stretched eastward until it covered my upper body. Coming out of a short doze, I opened my eyes and looked up to see the peak eclipsing the sun. A brilliant white flaming corona surrounded the top and sides of the upper mountain. I floated a few minutes longer until the sun had arched far enough west that I was again in its full glare.

Climbing into Quest's cockpit I greeted Wendy who had the charts of the Lesser Antilles spread before her.

"It looks like you've been busy" I said.

"We need to talk about something."

'What?"

"Do you know what day it is?"

"Your birthday?"

Quest in the Caribbean

"No. Today is July 31ˢᵗ" she said.

"Well then. Happy anniversary?" I said.

"Wrong" Wendy said. "It's going to be August 1ˢᵗ tomorrow. We have to get serious about hurricanes" she said holding up a colored printout of the hurricane tracks for the last fifty years.

"It's very colorful" I said.

"Come on, get serious. Aren't you scared of hurricanes?" she said.

"Not at the moment. Look, we're only about a hundred fifty miles from the south coast of Grenada" I said.

"I've got an idea" she said pointing at the chart. "We're right here. If we make a short stop in Bequia for a day or two, then Carriacou, we could be on the south shore of Grenada in less than a week."

"You're really making a big deal about nothing" I said.

"We better do something before it becomes a big deal" Wendy replied.

"You're right. Will it make you happy if we're in Clarkes Court Bay in a week?" I asked.

"Yes" Wendy said sitting down and letting out a big sigh.

"OK, we'll be in Grenada by next Sunday. Punch in waypoints here and here" I said marking the chart two miles east of St. Vincent. You'd better get some sleep. We'll leave August 1ˢᵗ."

"Great" she said clapping her hands.

We both dropped into the saloon.

Rastamen

"Drink this first. It will help you sleep" I said pouring two fingers of tequila in a tumbler.

"Straight? No way" she said pursing her lips.

"This ought to do it. It's enough for both of us" I said throwing it back. "Talk to you in a couple of weeks."

I walked into the forward berth to nap. I woke hours later. The boat was in pitch darkness and completely silent. My eyelids felt like they were glued shut and my tongue and throat were dry.

"Hey wake up Wendy" I said giving her a shove.

Wendy got up slowly, clicked on the red light and said "Your breath smells like old gym shoes."

"Thanks. Then get me some apple juice" I said. I swished the juice around in my mouth and swallowed. "Now we go" I said handing her the empty glass and pulling on my shorts.

As I felt my way to the bow in complete darkness, the cool night air raised goose bumps on my forearms. The bright, half moon had arched well past its zenith. Its white-blue light cast haunting shadows in the jungle on shore. The two Pitons loomed high above me. Their mist-shrouded peaks illuminated by the moonlight looked like mile-high phantoms. Placing the flashlight on the deck beside my knee I pulled the mooring pendant onto the deck. With a few well placed jabs from the marlin spike I managed to disentangle Quest's bowline from the pendant.

"We're free" I shouted into the darkness. A moment later, my voice echoed off the hills.

Wendy yelled back from the cockpit "OK, OK,OK".

Quest in the Caribbean

Quest was turned smartly to port until her bow was pointed into the middle of the bay. The sound of the engine echoing off the hills gradually grew fainter. We motored until we were a half mile off shore and the smell of diesel fumes blew straight into the cockpit.

"That's more like it" Wendy said when I shut down the engine.

The main and jib sheets were raised and trimmed for a night of light sailing.

"What's the course Captain?" Wendy said.

"We have a particularly good wind tonight. It's almost due west. I think we can make Bequia in one tack if we cut in very close to the west coast of St. Vincent. Move your first waypoint here, right off this place called Chateaubelair" I said pointing on the chart halfway down St. Vincent. "Then we should be able to sail the rest of the trip straight south to Port Elizabeth. I checked the weather fax this afternoon. Wind and sea are going to be mild with a gentle swell."

"Are we likely to have any surprises?" Wendy asked.

"No surprises tonight. I'll take the first watch" I said.

Wendy kissed me and disappeared into the dark cabin. As soon as she had turned off the lights, I took a comfortable prone position on the lee cockpit bench. With a rolled up windbreaker supporting my head, I pulled my cap over my eyes. Quest's mild yaw soon rocked me all the way to dreamland. I faded in and out of consciousness until being startled by a GPS alarm. Sitting up, I switched on the instrument panel light. 'What's going on here? This can't be right. We couldn't have sailed that far yet' I thought to myself. I reached into the lazarette for the handheld GPS and switched it on. When it acquired, I verified the position of the master GPS.

"Wendy" I yelled down into the cabin. "Get up here."

After finding her way through the dark cabin, Wendy rushed up the companionway pulling on a sweater. She jumped into the cockpit and said "What's wrong?"

"I don't think anything's wrong. We're at our first waypoint. We just sailed six hours and you didn't wake up. We're off the coast of St. Vincent. Look" I said pointing east.

Quest was about two miles off shore. The shacks that sprout from St. Vincent's hillsides were aglow with low watt incandescent light bulbs.

"It looks like we're at our waypoint. Let's make our tack now" I said loosening the jib sheet.

After releasing the main clutch brake, the sheet went slack. I turned the helm to port, altering our course to 180° due south.

"That was definitely the best sleep I've ever had on a night sail" Wendy said while she coiled the main sheet.

"That's about the best sleep I've ever had too" I said.

The false dawn was a leaden silvery glow in the eastern sky. The streaky, broken clouds that stretched low across the eastern horizon were just becoming ablaze with reds and oranges. The sun magically appeared sending flashes of sunlight glinting off the wave tops.

Quest in the Caribbean

"Look, it's Bequia" Wendy said pointing to the low hills that crown the small island.

Looking down at the instruments, I said "If our speed doesn't change, we should be there in about two hours."

Beginning another glorious and beautiful morning with all sails filled, we reached our Bequia waypoint around 09:30. After dropping the main and furling the jib, I let Quest drift peacefully in the turquoise water of the outer harbor.

"It looks pretty crowded. Where do you think we should anchor?" Wendy asked.

"That inner harbor looks full up. The swell isn't bad. Maybe somewhere out here along this beach" I said pointing two hundred yards in front of Quest.

We dropped the anchor and found excellent holding in twenty feet of water about a mile south of the village.

"Do you want to take another six hour nap before we check in?" Wendy asked joking.

"Not today. Let's get going" I said eagerly climbing over the lifelines into the dinghy.

Bequia's beautiful, well protected harbor and its close proximity to the very popular marine attractions of the Grenadines makes the island irresistible to both winter cruisers and the charter boat crowd. As we continued to motor deeper into the end of the bay, I was careful not to snag our prop on the mooring lines and anchor chains of the fleet of boats that crowded the bay close to the village. Arriving at the very popular city dock, Wendy pushed a couple of dinghies aside so that I could wedge the porta-bote into the mass of inflatables. Wendy jumped over two dinghies before adding our painter to the other ten painters that crowded the large iron dock cleat.

"Customs first?" Wendy asked as I stepped onto the dock.

We walked across the road and entered the charming old colonial Post Office which houses St. Vincent and the Grenadines Customs and Immigration. A bright friendly face greeted us as we stepped up to the window. Reaching out her hand, the woman accepted our papers and fee, smiled and welcomed us to Bequia.

"Excuse me ma'am, is there a vegetable market in town?" I asked as she returned our passports.

"Yes sir, it's down by the docks and you're in luck. Today is market day. Oh and by the way" she added, lowering her voice to a whisper. "You might have more luck buying from the ladies at the north end of the market. They'll give you the right price."

As we walked through the front door of the office I turned to Wendy. "What do you think she was getting at about the 'right price'?"

Wendy shrugged. "We're going to find out soon enough" she said.

We waited on the side of the road for two mini buses to pass before crossing over to the covered vegetable market. Just inside the entrance to the market sat a Rastafarian man arranging mangoes at a folding table. Separated from the Rasta by twenty feet were the women vendors who stood about their tables laughing and joking. Their tables were stacked with a bountiful arrangement of colorful fruits and vegetables from the nearby island of St. Vincent.

As I walked past the Rastafarian, he looked up and said "You want mango? Buy my mango."

"Sure man. Are they Julie mangoes?" I asked.

He ignored my question. I reached down and picked up a mango on top of the pile.

"Don't touch. You want mango, I pick for you" he said gruffly. He reached down and placed two green mangoes in a plastic bag. "Five dollar" he said holding the bag out in front of me.

"You've got to be kidding. I'll give you one dollar" I said.

The Rastafarian started on a slow burn. Then he erupted. "Get out of here" he shouted loud enough for the whole market to hear.

I shrugged and walked towards the women vendors. As we approached the first table, a friendly older woman gave me a broad welcoming smile.

Before I had a chance to say good morning the Rastafarian shouted across the market "You old women not going to sell him anything."

The entire group of women vendors turned their back to the Rasta in embarrassment. This was a good time for Wendy and me to make a fast departure.

As we made our way out the back of the market, a lady vendor cut us off. "You come back in couple hours when Rasta gone. We no fight with you. Rasta just mean. Come back. I sell you very good mangoes" she said with a welcoming smile.

"Thanks, we'll come back" I said smiling.

"It doesn't get much stranger than that" Wendy said as we continued up the dusty waterfront street. "Hey, there's the Bequia tourist bureau. Let's go in and pick up some brochures."

"Sure. It will be nice to take a break for a couple minutes" I said opening the door for Wendy.

We passed into the well appointed Bequia Tourism Association building and were greeted by two tall beautiful women with impeccable poise.

"You two must be models" I said smiling to the women.

They grinned and shyly asked if they could help us.

"I just want to look at the brochures" Wendy said walking up to the front desk.

"Help yourself. If I can find anything for you, just let me know" the taller of the women said.

While Wendy sorted through the brochure rack, I wandered towards a whale display at the back of the building. Turning around the back of the display, I was surprised to come face to face with a six foot five inch, disheveled Rastafarian mumbling gibberish to himself sitting on the floor.

"Morning" I said walking past.

The Rastafarian slowly straightened to his full height. He stared at me with fiery bloodshot eyes and said "Give me fifty bucks."

I drew myself up to my full but considerably shorter height. "Forget about it" I said.

He began to advance threateningly. "Hey. Dis not

America" he screamed in my face. "Dis Africa" he yelled pointing his index finger at the floor.

"You're right, this isn't America. But it's definitely not Africa. You're in the Caribbean. Now get lost" I said turning away.

The Tourism women heard the commotion and ran around the counter. When they saw the Rasta, they backed up and kept an appropriate distance.

"We call police" one of the women shouted at him.

The Rasta mumbled more unintelligible nonsense.

"Go now or police come to lock you up" the lady said to Rastaman.

He turned and began to stumble in the general direction of the door. Halfway to the door he slowly turned around, glared at me, pointed his finger and said "I get you."

The women rushed to my side like two over-protective mother ducks.

"Did he hurt you?" one of the women asked.

"Dis not the real Bequia" the other woman pleaded.

"I'm fine. Don't worry about it. This isn't my first bum encounter" I said shaking my head.

Wendy and I started walking to the door. The two tall women flanked me and continued to shower apologies.

"These things happen. Really. I'm more embarrassed for you two" I said stepping into the sunlight.

Wendy and I walked to the shade of a nearby tree and sat on a bench to compose ourselves. When our adrenaline levels were almost back to normal, we began a short walking tour of historic Port Elizabeth. Strolling the streets and alleys that date back to the 17th century gave us a brief glimpse into the hard lives of the early European settlers who had colonized the Grenadines. The island of Bequia enjoyed brief agricultural success with the production of coffee and indigo. Sugar cane was also cultivated for the production of rum. Bequia's very large and well protected harbor became one of the most important ship repair facilities in the southern Caribbean. A thriving and lucrative whaling industry was begun in 1875 by immigrants from Nantucket.

The killing of humpback whales in Bequia continues to the present. The International Whaling Commission sanctions the killing of four humpback whales in the waters around the island. The practice of whaling has understandably raised international concern from anti whaling organizations and conservation groups. The local tourism industry also takes a dim view of whaling in the Grenadines. Bequia whalers are adamant about continuing their humpback whale hunting. As local whaler Kingsley Stowe says "Whaling is our tradition here in Bequia. We will continue to whale, and we'll continue the tradition."

Twenty

Home free

The island of Bequia was a most pleasant and
hospitable place to lay back and spend a few days. After we
had provisioned and explored the lovely island it was time
to journey south. Our goal of sailing to the southern shore
of Grenada would soon be realized. With great anticipation
we raised the anchor and sailed out of Admiralty Bay on a
feather light breeze. The golden early morning sunlight
intensified the saturated blues and oranges of the pirogues
that hugged the shoreline. No one could be seen moving in
the village. The only sign of life was a small pack of village
mongrels that wandered aimlessly about the vegetable
market hoping for a discarded scrap. A single hawk circled
above the hills. With silence all around us and Quest barely
inching forward in the light air the world seemed to be
moving in slow motion. Wendy was busy in the cockpit
finalizing our waypoints when I came through the
companionway with a bowl of mango fruit salad.

"I bet you're glad we went back to the fruit market
yesterday" I said.

Wendy picked up a fork and speared a mango slice.
"I'm even more glad that the Rasta wasn't there" she said.

Home free

"Which one?"

"Both" she replied.

The full force of the trade wind finally caught up to us. We made our port tack after rounding the rocky reefs that extend far out on Bequia's western side. Following a course of 180° and with the sails trimmed taut, Wendy and I leaned back in the cockpit to enjoy our pleasure cruise through the southern Grenadines.

"Did you hear that bump on the bow? I think we have visitors" I said getting up to take a look.

"I did hear something" Wendy said.

Edging along the windward rail, I stepped around the head sails and advanced to the bowsprit. Quest hobby horsed through a mild head sea at a considerable six knots. I steadied myself at the bow pulpit as Quest charged forward through the waves. White froth and jets of cool spray flew over the bow platform as she plunged and rose.

"Wendy, you've got to see this" I yelled back to the cockpit.

"Be right there" she answered.

Wendy crept up the leeward side and ducked under the sails.

"Watch yourself, it's a bit slippery" I said as she stepped nearer to me.

I helped her over the windlass. I reached out and tugged her forward. Extending an embracing arm about her waist I held her tightly against the bow pulpit.

"Look" I said pointing.

The silvery flash of a long bottle-nose dolphin appeared and streaked in front of the bow. A second large dolphin raced from the opposite direction, breached and did a back flip twenty feet in front of the bow.

"Here comes the rest of the family" Wendy said pointing halfway along Quest's lee rail to where a pod of ten smaller dolphins and a half dozen pups raced along in Quest's wake.

The first two dolphins had taken up positions on each side of the bow and appeared to be swimming in competition.

"What a game" Wendy said. "I bet they're having fun."

"It does look like a fun game. I'm not sure it's all fun though" I said.

"What do you mean?" Wendy asked.

"Keep watching. You'll see" I said. "Watch the one on the right. I think he's getting ready to make his move."

The starboard dolphin abruptly turned to the left and drove his snout into the underbelly of the dolphin on the left. The bumped dolphin dove deep letting out a stream of bubbles while the aggressor did a victory dance along the side of Quest on his rear fluke. Within a moment the two sparring dolphins were right back at it, racing the bow wave together and carrying on their bump and chase game. The competition reached its climax when the two dolphins each began to leap higher and higher out of the water in front of the bowsprit.

"I bet they don't stay much longer. Look over there" I said pointing to a school of flying fish skimming over waves fifty feet off our port side.

The dolphins' exhibition immediately terminated.

The entire pod all turned simultaneously to the left and raced off in pursuit of the school of flying fish. After the two gladiator dolphins and their fan club abandoned Quest's bow for a quick snack of flying fish, we returned to the cockpit.

Wendy turned to me and said "It must be nice to be able to play in the Caribbean all day."

"It is" I replied.

Within two hours of leaving Admiralty Bay we had made remarkable progress charging through the neon blue waters of the Grenadines under full sail. Ninety degrees off our port beam and only five miles away was the small, secluded and very secretive island appropriately named Mustique. Before it became the exclusive destination for European royalty and friends, the island was no more than a barren rock in a beautiful ocean. Today it is the only privately owned island in the Grenadines, purchased by Baron Glencooner in 1958 for the unimaginable sum of £45,000. In 1960 the entire island was immediately transformed from a shrub strewn rock pile that was unable to support even a small herd of dwarf sheep into the Caribbean's number one playground for the world's royalty. Within a year, multi-million dollar villas sprouted on this desert island like over-watered dandelions. The secret island of Mustique had such influential friends in rarefied circles that it did not even appear on maps. As soon as the linen, silverware and vintage champagne were delivered, European royalty immediately embraced the island as one of the few places in the world where they 'could let their hair down and be themselves'. Nothing as big as a small

Quest in the Caribbean

island could stay secret for long. Unfortunately for the
royals, by 1980 the island was beginning to be over run with
billionaire commoners also trying to let their hair down.
Today sighting of royalty on Mustique is rarer than spotting
a mountain gorilla in a Manhattan subway. Yet the rooms
are a very affordable $3000 a night not including tax and
gratuities. Stay in the Princess room and don't forget to
order a glass of the Krug Clos d'Ambonnay.

The Grenadines stretch south from St. Vincent all
the way to Grenada and are comprised of thirty two islands
and cays. Only nine are inhabited. The ethnic composition
of the Grenadines is unique. Columbus first sailed past the
island group on his fourth voyage in 1502. The Carib
Indians had occupied the islands for over thirteen hundred
years. Columbus and his armada of conquistadors largely
ignored the Grenadines to concentrate on Indian genocide
and plundering gold and silver in Central and South
America. In the late 1600's a freak storm and a strange twist
of fate wrecked a very large Dutch ship holding 3000 slaves
on the shores of St. Vincent. The imprisoned cargo
overpowered their masters and liberated themselves,
escaping to the neighboring islands in the Grenadines. They
soon interbred with the islands' Carib and Arawak
inhabitants to form an ethnic group known as the
Garifuna. The uniqueness of the Garifuna language is in its
use of loanwords or words borrowed from other languages.
In Garifuna, men and women can use separate
vocabularies. Men use words borrowed from the warring
Carib, whereas women use the more peace-oriented Arawak
vocabulary.

214

Home free

The Grenadines were colonized around 1796, much later than the rest of the Caribbean. African slaves toiled for a few years on British plantations producing sugar, coffee, indigo, tobacco, cotton and cocoa. The economy went into the normal period of decline in the early 1800's. During this time of lost fortunes, the landowners abandoned their estates and slaves. In 1838 slaves were fully emancipated in the Grenadines.

A very steady fifteen knot trade wind and a sawtooth-shaped sea gave us a very fast, bumpy ride past the small, sparsely populated islands of Canouan, Mayreau and Union. By two o'clock in the afternoon we had come within sight of Carriacou. Before we could set the anchor in Tyrrel Bay on the western coast, it was necessary to make a short detour to Customs which is housed in the main city of Hillsborough on the other side of the island. The Customs house in Hillsborough serves as the most northern port of entry for Grenada.

"We're almost there" I said to the Customs officer as he handed us our stamped passports.

"Almost where?" he asked smiling.

"About forty more miles and we'll be home" I said giving Wendy a quick glance.

He looked at our passports a second time. "Oh. You two must be on your way to hide out on da south shore. We get a lot of boaters passing south dis time of year" he said smiling.

"Thanks" I said taking the passports.

Wendy and I pushed through the single door of the office and raced each other to the dinghy dock. Within forty-five minutes we had motored Quest the short distance around the west coast of Carriacou to the very well sheltered Tyrrel Bay. Entering the anchorage from the north corner I scanned the busy harbor for an empty spot.

"You're not going to believe this. I think I just spotted Jean Pierre and Laura's boat close to the haul out dock" I said.

"Pull up so we can say hi" Wendy said.

Before we got within thirty feet of their boat, Pierre and Laura spotted us and waved enthusiastically. I dropped the anchor one hundred feet off to one side of them and let out enough chain to bring our boats side by side.

"It's great to see you" Pierre said.

"Come over when you're settled so we can catch up" Laura added.

We made short work of covering the sail and squaring away the decks. Wendy chose a good bottle of wine and we paddled over.

"We haven't seen you since Puerto Rico" Laura said beaming as she hugged both of us twice.

"Come sit down and have something to eat" Pierre said motioning to the raw vegetables that he had spread out on the cockpit table.

The evening flew by with each of us recounting our adventures since we last met. When fatigue finally caught up to me I got up to leave.

"So where are you staying for hurricane season?" Pierre asked.

"Wendy made reservations at Clarke's Court Marina when we were in Hillsborough this morning" I said.

Home free

"We've been to Clarke's Court. It's good" Laura said.

"At least it's below 12 degrees" I said.

"When it comes to hurricanes don't count on anything" Pierre said prophetically.

"So where are you two staying this season?" I asked.

"Well" Pierre said stealing a glance at Laura. "Above 12 degrees. The boat's staying here in Tyrrel Bay. I'm waiting on an injector pump. We're going back to Montreal for a few months."

"Come see us on the south shore" I said.

The anchorage was still and dark. Stepping over the rail, the star saturated night sky reflected off the water. I felt like I was stepping into the sky. Motoring up to Quest's side, the bright half moon rose low on the horizon silhouetting her profile. After climbing the swim ladder I gave our friends a final wave.

That night I tossed and turned in our berth like tomorrow was the Fourth of July. The next morning both Wendy and I were up with the sun. With no ceremony or fanfare, the anchor was raised and pinned.

"Are you ready to see our new home today? It's only fifty miles straight down there" I said pointing.

"I'm ready" Wendy said.

Dreams and plans that we had nurtured for more than four years were becoming real. All the storms, bad anchorages and minor inconveniences were no more than forgotten inconsequential moments as we sailed out of Tyrrel Bay. Walking to the bow I looked south to the high volcanic peaks of Grenada. How often had I planned and dreamed of making Grenada our tropical paradise? How often had these dreams almost eluded us?

By lunchtime we were off the city of St. George's, the capital of Grenada. A strong off shore breeze carried the earthy, tropical fragrance of the Spice Island out to Quest pulling us ever closer to our dream.

Sitting in the cockpit holding hands, excited as a couple of newlyweds, I turned to Wendy and said "Some times I wonder what we're doing here. A few years ago we didn't know a bow from a prow. Remember leaving Riviera Beach last year and sailing into the Gulf stream?"

"I remember being terrified when the coast of Florida disappeared" Wendy said.

"How about when we left Georgetown and sailed into that twenty-five foot sea? We're having some good times. Do you think we'll like Grenada?" I asked.

"Probably."

After passing St George's our course was altered to sail along the pristine beaches that stretch southeast.

At the end of the cape, Wendy yelled "There's the airport."

"Let's get ready for our tack" I said as we glided past the southwest tip of Grenada.

We both stood up and with skills honed daily for the last year we made our tack and headed east. Luckily there were no mishaps.

"That must be St. Georges University" I said was we passed the Grenada airport.

"It says in the guide that the airport has the longest runway in the Caribbean. It's over two miles long and can land a 747" Wendy said.

A half mile down the coast a very strong head sea began to bash Quest's bow and ship a substantial amount of green water onto her foredeck. While passing the very busy and rolly Prickly Bay I looked into the anchorage.

"I'm glad we're not stopping there tonight. That doesn't look like much fun" I said pointing to the fleet of masts that wagged violently at anchor.

"It does look a bit rough" Wendy agreed.

"I don't think we're going to have that problem in Clarke's Court Marina. Look on the chart here. Clarke's Court Bay looks much more protected by all these offshore islands" I said.

"That's funny. When I called the marina yesterday, that's exactly what Bob the owner told me."

"Let's hope he's right" I said.

The southern shore of Grenada is deeply indented by a series of mile-deep fjords surrounded by steep hillsides. Wendy and I couldn't take our eyes off the beautiful coastline with its mysterious deep blue bays and hills covered by tropical flowers.

"Wow. This is paradise and what's even better we're finally safe. Hurricanes can't get us now" I said.

"That's Mount Hartman Bay" Wendy shouted happily.

"We should start looking for the channel to Clarke's Court Bay" I said.

"Oh yeah, I forgot to tell you. Bob at the marina told me one of the big developers just put in a big buoy marking the entrance. He said to to make sure that we put the buoy on our right, then steer a straight course to the docks" Wendy said.

"That's sounds pretty simple. There are a couple of shoals we have to avoid. It doesn't look too bad. There it is. I can see the buoy."

I lowered the sails, turned the engine on and turned left. We were home free at last.

The End

www.questandcrew.com

Recipe Index

From 'Quest in the Caribbean'

From 'Quest and Crew'

From 'Quest on the Thorny Path'

From 'Quest for the Virgins'

*

Made in the USA
Columbia, SC
01 November 2022

70306229R10136